GW00746234

Freshwater fishing
in South Africa

This book is especially
for my sons Jeffrey and Paul

FRESHWATER FISHING IN SOUTH AFRICA

Michael G. Salomon

The complete guide to fresh water fishing

Chris van Rensburg Publications (Pty) Ltd
P.O. Box 25272 Ferreirasdorp 2048 Johannesburg
Republic of South Africa

First Edition 1978
ISBN 0 908393 23 7

Foreword

Angling is by far the most popular sport in South Africa today and the challenge of fly-fishing in particular is resulting in more and more anglers giving up bait and spinners and taking up fly tackle. Expert salt-water fly fishermen have even landed bill-fish and huge sharks on fly and every type of freshwater fish (except eel and moggel) mentioned in this book can be caught on fly.

Nothing has given me so much pleasure, peace of mind and delight, as the hours I have spent with rod and reel. The challenge of most types of fishing is both physical and intellectual. I can do no better than quote the words of James Rennie who, way back in 1883, wrote that "angling is a sport that requires as much enthusiasm as poetry, as much patience as mathematics and as much caution as housebreaking".

There is much more to fishing than the mere, catching of a fish. There is the enjoyment of natural beauty and one's surroundings, whether it be the splendour of the Drakensberg mountains or the sparkle and rapture of a fast flowing stream, or the tranquillity of the still water of a lake or dam. There is the weary satisfaction after a long day spent wading in rugged rivers and through dense undergrowth. There is the feeling of isolation, being away from the hurly-burly, and inner peace which comes from being alone with nature.

It gives me great pleasure to welcome the publication of this complete guide for the South African freshwater angler. Such an omnibus vademecum has been long overdue and I am sure the entie angling fraternity, both beginner and old hand, will find it both revealing and fascinating reading. The book not only tells how to fish but where to fish. The author goes into minute and enlightening detail on the variety of hooks, bait and techniques used to catch the various types of fish. The text is enlivened by graphic descriptions of the memorable experiences of some renowned members of the angling fraternity and is well illustrated with drawings and photographs. Reference is also made to the latest South African records. Particular attention has been given to the latest methods and techniques of fly fishing.

This long awaited book will be eagerly seized by both aspiring and established anglers.

Trevor Babich

Acknowledgments

The author is especially grateful to Pat Hendley, Bill Steele, Royce Rosettenstein, Trevor Babich, Graham Barrett and Geoff Knipe for their invaluable contributions to this book.

Design
Colin Bridgeford, Insight Graphics, Pretoria

Photography, back cover
B. Martin

Photo typesetting
Pointset (Pty) Ltd, Johannesburg

Lithographic reproduction
McManus Bros (Pty) Ltd, Cape Town

Printers
Hortors Printers, Johannesburg

Publishers
Chris van Rensburg Publications (Pty) Ltd
P.O. Box 25272
Ferreirasdorp, 2048
Telephone 726-4350
Johannesburg

Preface

Angling is by far the most popular sport in South Africa today. In fact, over 142 000 fishing licenses, excluding 2 200 trout licences, were taken out by law-abiding anglers in the Transvaal alone during 1977. This figure excludes children under the age of 16 years who are not required to buy a licence. Many inland anglers are unaware of the variety of good fishing which many dams and rivers afford, and this book has been written for their benefit as well as to assist the beginner.

Contrary to common belief luck plays a minor role in angling. There is a great deal of skill involved and over the years the experienced angler will have learned the habits, haunts and preferences of a particular type of fish, the manner in which they bite, the choice of baits to use, and other important factors such as water and temperature conditions.

The larger specimens which we all dream of hooking have become so because they are cautious and have acquired a number of conditioned reflexes as a result of experience. For example, a large fish once hooked on a paste bait is unlikely to take such a bait for the following two or three seasons. The more cautious a fish is, the greater its chances of survival, and this is why relatively few records are broken although there are ever increasing numbers of anglers and fishing tackle is improved all the time. I visited a small private dam near Barberspan during a recent dry season. The dam was rapidly drying up and the farmer was netting the fish in it. The fishing there had generally been regarded as poor, and I was therefore amazed to see ton upon ton of fish netted, including many carp weighing over 15 kg, barbel over 20 kg, and yellow-fish of over 10 kg. To catch large fish takes experience and the angler must take steps to allay their fear and suspicion and then, having been fortunate enough to hook a big fish, the angler has to test his skill in playing and landing it. Fish are unpredictable, however, and no angler can lay down hard and fast rules as to what should be done in a particular set of circumstances, and the information contained in this book should be viewed in this light.

I hope that the aspirant angler, after reading this book, will have gained sufficient knowledge to assist him in developing this sport to a fine art.

Contents

1

What fishing requires of the angler

Fishing Regulations
Licence

All anglers over the age of 16 years must each year take out a provincial angling licence (obtainable from the Receiver of Revenue and most sport shops stocking fishing tackle). This entitles them to fish in any water, whether public or private, in that province. (This does not apply to the owner or occupier of land on which there is water). The permission of the person who has the angling rights over such water must also be obtained before you may fish there.

Permits, which must be signed by you, must also be obtained before you may fish in forest and Bantu reserves. In addition, a special licence must be purchased to fish for trout. An angler is obliged by law to produce his licence on demand to any authorised person, so you must carry it with you whenever you go fishing.

Transvaal
Undersized fish and bag limits

A fish measuring less than the length given in the schedule below must be returned to the water immediately and carefully:

Species of fish	Bag limits per day	Length in centimetres
Bass	6	20
Yellow-fish (including Silver Fish, White Fish and Kalwerkop)	10	30
Tiger Fish	6	30
Kurper	20	15
Trout	6	20

A fish is correctly measured on a horizontal plane: one takes the distance from the tip of the snout to the fork of its tail.

Trout licence

There is now no closed season. The licence fee is R6,00 p.a. per calendar year.

Bag limits

An angler may not exceed the bag limits per day in respect of the fish referred to in the above schedule.

Ground-baiting

Catching fish by making a feeding area is prohibited in certain areas.

Jigging

Fish can be caught in the body by tying a number of hooks to the line and jerking them through the water. This practice, known as jigging, is prohibited. In spring, kurper will be found in their thousands just below the surface of the water, carrying spawn in their mouths, which they release after seven to ten days, and only then will they start feeding. Whilst they are so spawning they can easily be foul-hooked by jigging. This practice is illegal and unsporting in the extreme.

Fish nets or traps and pollution of water	It is an offence to catch fish with a fish net or trap and to deposit any substance in the water which may be injurious to fish.
Number of lines and hooks	An angler may not use more than two lines, and to each may be attached not more than two single hooks with natural bait; or two single trout or bass flies; or one artificial lure or spoon.
Live bait	Live bait *i.e.* small live fish may not be used for bait.
Cape Province	In terms of the Nature Conservation Ordinance no. 19 of 1974 and Regulations P.N.955/75, effective from 1 September 1975, angling licences are required for fishing in all fresh waters of the Cape Province, but not in tidal waters. Angling licences do not entitle holders to catch fish without the permission of the owner of the water, whether a government department, local authority or private owner.
Trout	Trout are protected by a closed season, a size limit and daily bag limit. Where only the use of non-spinning artificial fly is permitted, this is defined as a hook with one point and one barb to which matter not edible by fish is attached and which is constructed so that it will not rotate when drawn through the water and to which no appliance is affixed which is capable of rotating or spinning round. There is no limit to the size of the fly.
Black bass	Bass have no closed season, but are protected by size and daily bag limits.
Landing nets	Although no person shall in any fresh waters use any net, speargun or other appliance which can be used for catching fish (unless he is the holder of a special permit), a landing net with an opening not exceeding 610 mm is permitted for lifting out fish caught by angling.
Trout areas	The principal trout fishing areas are scheduled as 'trout areas' in which anglers may not catch *any kind of fish* without a licence and only with the non-spinning artificial fly. Forty-five trout areas are scheduled with a closed season from 2 June to 31 August every year, except where otherwise proclaimed.
Reservoirs	The following are trout areas where the use of a spinning fly or lure (as well as the prescribed artificial fly) is permitted for catching trout: Wemmershoek Dam, Bethel Dam, Nantes Dam, Steenbras Reservoir and Stettynskloof Dam. There is no closed season in Wemmershoek Dam. Steenbras Reservoir has a municipal closed season from 1 September to 30 November.
Licence fee	The fee for angling licences for inland waters, other than tidal waters, is R1,00 for a calendar year. These are obtained from a Receiver of Revenue. There are now no other categories of angling licences.

Trout open season	1 September to 1 June.
Size limits	Length measured in a straight line along the side of the fish from the end of the nose to the furthermost point of the tail: Trout, all species, 230 mm; Black bass, all species, 250 mm; Yellow-fish, Clanwilliam yellow-fish *Barbus capensis*, 400 mm; Large-mouth Yellow-fish, Orange River system series, *Barbus kimberleyensis*, 300 mm.
Daily bag limit	No person shall catch more than ten fish per day.

Orange Free State

In terms of the Nature Conservation Ordinance (no. 8 of 1969) no person shall among other things:

☐ Promote or hold an angling competition except in terms of a permit issued by the Administrator

☐ Participate in an unauthorised angling competition

☐ Use a fixed line to angle

☐ fish:– (A) with more than two lines; (B) other than with a single hook; (C) with a line to which more than two single hooks are attached; (D) with more than one spoon or other artificial bait in lieu of two single hooks

☐ Import into or sell any live freshwater fish in the province, except in terms of a permit issued by the Administrator

☐ Keep any fish of the species shown in the following list, which is less than the minimum length stated (measured from the tip of the snout to the fork of the tail), but shall immediately return such fish to the water: Black bass (20 cm); and Yellow-fish (30 cm)

☐ Catch and keep more fish of the following species than the number shown: Bass (6) and Yellow-fish (10)

☐ Use live fish for bait

☐ Angle without having a licence on his or her person.

Natal

Angling waters are of two types: trout waters and non-trout waters.

Trout waters are listed in a proclamation which lays down the limits of each trout water in Natal. Any water which is not listed in Schedule A of the proclamation is, legally, a non-trout water, even if it does contain trout. Conversely, anyone fishing in scheduled trout waters is subject to all the applicable regulations, whether the fish being caught are trout or other species. It should be noted that each scheduled trout water includes all tributaries. Water impounded by a dam on a side-stream is therefore subject to the same closed season and other restrictions as the river into which the stream flows.

The open season for most trout waters is 1 September to 15 May, but some are open throughout the year.

Bag and size limits

The general limits for trout are 10 fish per day, of a minimum length of 200 mm, but the current regulations should be consulted, because there are exceptions.

Tackle

In trout waters, anglers, may use only artificial non-spinning flies tied on single hooks, not exceeding 40 mm in length. It is illegal to use any form of artificial lure other than a non-spinning fly. No natural bait is permitted. Fixed-spool reels are prohibited on all trout waters.

Waters which are not scheduled trout waters are open for angling throughout the year.

Tackle

Any type of hook or lure may be used, provided not more than three hooks are attached to one line (a double or treble hook is counted as one hook), and provided each angler uses not more than two lines.

Lines may not be left unattended for more than one hour. If they are left for longer periods, they are considered to be 'set lines' which are illegal.

There are no restrictions on the type of bait which may be used, except that if live fish are to be used for bait, the live fish may not be brought from some other source, but must be taken from the actual water being fished. This is to prevent the accidental transfer of undesirable species.

Bag and size limits

There is no restriction on the taking of small bass, but not more than 12 bass of 225 mm and over may be taken by an angler in one day.

A limit of 15 scalies or yellow-fish applies to all non-trout waters. In the Buffalo, White Umfolozi and Pongola rivers there is an additional restriction in that no scalies of less than 250 mm in length may be taken.

To determine the length of any fish, including trout, the measurement shall be made in a straight line from the tip of the snout to the end of the central rays of the tail fin.

There are no limits in respect of size or number for other freshwater fish in Natal.

Licences

There are three types of licence:

☐ General fishing licence, costing R3 for adults or R1,50 for juveniles under 16 years. This is valid for trout waters AND non-trout waters throughout the province for a maximum period of one year

☐ Temporary fishing licence, costing R1 for adults or 50 cents for juveniles and also valid for all waters but only for eight consecutive days

☐ Bass, bluegill and indigenous fishing licence, costing R1 for adults or 50 cents for juveniles. This is valid for non-trout waters for a period of one year

Licences are obtainable from Receivers of Revenue and from authorised issuing officers at sports shops and hotels. Licences are not transferable.

Fishing
competitions

To organise or participate in an angling competition is illegal without the consent of the Administrator. Only registered angling

The author with two Tilapia mossambica in the 1,5 kg class caught at Hartbeespoort Dam on earthworms

clubs or associations may obtain permission to stage competitions.

Sale of fish

A special licence or permit is required to sell trout, but freshwater fish of any other kind may be sold by anyone who has obtained the fish lawfully.

**General Note
Keeping fishing
spots clean**

It is very important to keep fishing spots clean for both your own benefit and enjoyment and that of other anglers. Do not break bottles or leave bottle tops or tins at the water's edge. These may seriously injure an unfortunate angler wading in the water when it has risen. Livestock will eat old plastic bags which may cause their death; or they may stray through gates left open. The landowner may then withhold angling privileges not only to your detriment but to that of all anglers.

13

2　The angler's requirements

Take care in selecting your tackle. If well looked after, your rod and reel will serve you well for many years. If you do not know what type of tackle to buy for your particular requirements, seek the guidance and advice of an old hand or an enthusiastic and reliable dealer. A rod with a stiff action cannot absorb the shock of a plunging fish, and the line will break more easily. You will also find that a larger rod is more advantageous when you fish with a float or over a river-bed in an area full of snags.

The test curve of a rod is also important. To ascertain this, suspend a spring-balance from the end ring of the rod. While you hold the butt of the rod, someone should pull the spring-balance to the point where the tip of the rod is at an angle of 90° to the butt. The spring-balance should have the following approximate readings for the fish mentioned: Carp (0,68 kg), Yellow-fish and general fishing (0,56 kg), and Barbel (1,13 kg). A trout rod is chosen for its action, not its test curve.

You should also choose a hollow rather than a solid glass-fibre rod, as the lighter weight makes it easier and more comfortable to use. Modern carbon fibre rods represent the ultimate in up-to-date design. They are, however, very expensive.

Rods for river and dam fishing

To achieve satisfaction in your angling, you should select a light rod 2 to 3 metres in length or 3,5 m for float-fishing. It must be flexible and have a good action. If the rod is too rigid the strain will be on the eyes or rod rings instead of on the rod. This will cause the line to break more easily and you will be deprived of much of the enjoyment of the sport when playing the fish.

Light tackle

Both the beginner and the experienced angler will find that the best results are obtained with light tackle. The longer and more flexible the rod, the further and more easily you can cast with it. If you use heavy tackle and try to haul in a fish by brute force, the strain of the fish on one end and you on the other, will usually break the line at a frayed section, knot or other weak point, or the hook may be torn out of the fish's mouth, particularly if it was not well hooked. If you fish with light tackle, however, you will be obliged to allow the fish to run when it chooses to do so. This is where your skill in guiding and controlling the fish comes into play: you must pit your wits against the instinct and fear that the fish will show, and be able to anticipate each desperate run and turn as the fish seeks an underwater obstruction in its bid for freedom. You know that if you use too much force the fish will break your line. This is where skill in playing a fish comes into play. When the fish is finally exhausted and brought to your net, you will know you have fought it on even terms and won because of your skill. A well designed rod also acts as a shock absorber to sudden plunges.

Using light tackle you will hook and land more fish, and find that the lure looks and moves more naturally in clearer water. Also, a fish taking a bait will feel less resistance and, therefore, take it more readily. The larger fish are very wary and generally bite gently, and will leave the bait if they feel any resistance. You will also detect and feel bites more easily.

Suitable line

Soft lines tend to become springy and easily tangle and develop kinks. They will also deteriorate more quickly as a result of ultra-violet radiation from the sunlight. You should select a dark line with a finer diameter than other lines with the same breaking strain. This will enable you to cast further as there is less resistance. You can dye a line with a 10 per cent silver nitrate solution. Fish do not detect a dark line as easily. A line with 2 to 3,5 kg breaking strain is ideal for carp, kurper, bass, yellow-fish, silver-fish and muddies. A line with a 4 to 4,5 kg breaking strain should be used for barbel.

A fish of up to 1,5 kg (particularly a carp which is not a great fighter) can be landed fairly easily on a 2 to 3 kg line if it is played correctly. The sport and satisfaction of angling lies in landing a large fish with light tackle. There is no achievement in catching a 0,5 kg fish on a 6 kg line. The experienced angler should be able to land a fish weighing three or four times the equivalent of the breaking strain of the line. I recently witnessed an ultra-light enthusiast fight and land, after a battle lasting over 9 hours, a skate weighing some 75 kg on a line having a breaking strain of only 6,5 kg. Whenever the fish tired and clung to the ocean bottom, as they are accustomed to do, the angler would pluck his rod whilst keeping it up and the line taut, thus sending vibrations along it which caused the fish to swim off again. This technique has also been successfully used on barbel and especially vundu, which also lie on the bottom of the river or dam when they become tired and only move off to continue the fight when they have rested.

The specific gravity of a fish is similar to that of water so that a fish in water may be regarded as almost weightless. This explains why an angler is able to play a heavy fish in the water on a line with a breaking strain a fraction of the weight of the fish, and why the line would break if the fish were to be lifted out of the water.

Reels

A beginner should choose an open-face reel or fixed-spool reel, as this type is easy to handle and cast with, and prevents overwinds or 'birds' nests'. It is worth investing in a good rod and reel which should last many years. The weight of the reel should be in proportion to that of the rod, so that you are not conscious of extra weight when holding your rod and reel. The drag should in fact be set to the test curve of the rod, so that it will give when the tip of the rod is pulled to an angle of 90° to the butt. Ensure that the reel is firmly secured to the rod. If not, it will fall off when you cast or work itself loose when you are fighting a sizeable fish. Before you start fishing, adjust your drag so that the line can be pulled out fairly easily under pressure. Do not wind too much line on to your spool. With an overfull spool the line will recoil when you cast, causing a tangle. You should leave a space of approximately 2 mm between the last layer of line and the outer curve of the spool. The correct tension setting comes with practice, but the line must not be capable of being pulled out too easily, else the fish will not tire and you will not be able to exercise control. If the drag is set too tight, as is often the case, the sudden run of a hooked fish will break the line, or a rod left unattended can be pulled into the water.

When I first started angling I used to tighten the drag on the reel and release the ratchet so that the handle could turn freely both backwards and forwards, believing that if I hooked a large fish which I could not control, I would be able to simply take my hand off the handle of the reel and allow the fish to run freely, and when its run was over I would wind it in.

The day came when I was spinning for tiger fish and had landed several small specimens. I lazily flicked out the small spoon I was using and slowly retrieved it. Suddenly I felt a tremendous pull which caused the freely moving handle to swing back violently and hit my fingers. The impact was so great that the handle broke off and the line peeled out uncontrolled. Nursing my injured fingers I helplessly watched a gigantic tiger fish climb out of the river and throw the spoon out of its mouth.

After that experience, I now carefully check before I start fishing – and every now and then while fishing – that the drag is correctly set and the ratchet on, neither too loose nor too tight. I believe that a right-handed person should use a left-handed reel: he is then able to use his right hand to hold the rod and thus have more control.

Sinkers

Use as light a sinker as possible and always have available a selection of sinkers of various sizes. If you can avoid using a sinker, e.g. by using a heavy paste bait, so much the better. Your choice of sinker will be governed by the particular water conditions and the type of bait you use. If you are fishing with a paste bait in a dam, a very light sinker may be used, particularly if it is a calm day. If a brisk wind is blowing, a light sinker will be unsuitable, as the paste bait will fall to pieces once the line is moved about. Similarly, a heavier sinker will have to be used in a fast-moving river, else the bait will be brought to the surface. The sole function of the sinker is to enable you to cast out your bait, take it to the bottom and keep your line in position. Some anglers incorrectly believe that if they use a heavy sinker, the fish will hook itself and won't have to be struck. It is the action of the rod and the drag that hooks the fish, however, not the sinker.

How many sinkers are lost, depends to a large extent upon the type used. A flat or round sinker is more likely to become caught on a rocky bottom than a spoon-shaped sinker which tends to lift rather than drag along the bottom when it is pulled. When you fish in a weedy area you should change to a barrel-shaped sinker which, being tapered, can be pulled through the weeds more easily.

One of the best designed sinkers is barrel-shaped, with a swivel embedded at one end. The line is passed through the

The beautiful Crocodile River, Dullstroom

The author and Pat Hendley kurper fishing at
Hartbeespoort Dam

swivel eye and a lead shot is used as a 'stop'. This running sinker rig is extremely sensitive.

Hooks

The design of hooks varies as regards length, bend and point angle. A small hook is invariably preferable to a large hook. Size 4 or 5 is a good all-round size for river and dam fishing. Recommended hook sizes for each type of fish are dealt with more fully in the relevant chapters.

Trace

The breaking strain of the line used as a trace for the hook should be slightly lower than that of the main line so that the trace but not the line will break under strain when an underwater obstruction is hooked. If your fishing spot has a number of underwater obstacles and you are prepared to lose sinkers, you should also use a weaker trace to secure your sinker to your line.

Bait

As a general rule, keep your bait small. A large piece of bait may on occasion tempt a very large fish, but a large fish will just as readily, if not more so, take a small bait, and with small bait the angler has the opportunity at the same time of catching smaller fish which would be unable to take the large bait. It is interesting to note that the world record for a carp caught on rod and line (with a breaking strain of under 2,7 kg) is 22,34 kg. This fish was caught in the Transvaal on a bait consisting of a single maize pip.

Angler's knots in nylon

It goes without saying that it is very important to know how to tie the correct knots when assembling your tackle. A bad knot is the usual cause of a line breaking. The angler must be able to tie a hook to a trace and the trace and sinker to the line. He must be able to join two pieces of line. When spinning, the lure must be tied to the line. It may be necessary to tie a swivel on to your line. There are several different knots for each of these requirements, and the following have proved very satisfactory when correctly tied.

To gut a hook
The Shank Whip

Cut a length of trace some 60 cm and thread the one end (A) through the eye of the hook and along the front of the shank so that it rests halfway down the shank. Hold this end against the shank and then thread the eye with the other end of the trace (B) from the opposite side so that the trace forms a loop.

With your one hand hold the bottom of the loop at point (C) together with the end of the line (A) against the shank, and with your other hand take the loop at point (D) and wind it four to six times round the shank and the end of the line (A) below the eye of the hook. Then pull the other end of the line (B) tight.

In order to tie a loop in the gutted line to connect it to your main line, tie an ordinary knot approximately 2,5 cm from the end of the line. Make a loop in the line and bring the end of the loop twice through the first loop. Tighten the line and the loop will slide up to the knot. You now have a perfectly gutted hook.

To tie a swivel, clip or hook to your line
The Clinch knot

Thread the end of the line through the eye of the swivel; bring it back and twist it at least four times around the main line.

Then thread the end through the loop next to the eye; hold the end and pull the main line tight.

This knot can be further improved upon. Before pulling the knot tight, pass the end of the line through the last loop formed around the main line; then pull the knot tight. This is known as a Tucked Clinch.

The Pigtail knot

The illustration shows why the knot bears this name. It is easier to tie the knot if a match-stick is laid alongside the eye of the swivel or hook and the line threaded through the eye and around the match. The match is removed before the line is pulled tight.

If the eye of your hook is turned up or down, an easily tied knot can be made by pushing one end of the line through the eye of the hook, winding it tightly around the shank five or six times and then threading the end of the line through the loop closest to the eye. Pull on the main line to tighten the knot. Ensure that the eye of the hook is properly closed before tying this knot.

It is advisable to tie a slip-knot in the end of the line before making any of these knots.

To join two ends of line
The Blood knot

This is the best knot I know when the diameters of the two strands are approximately the same. Here is the easy step-by-step way of tying it.

1. Lap the ends of the strands to be joined and twist one around the other, making at least five turns. Count the turns made. Place the end between the strands, following the arrow.

2. Hold the end against the turns already made, between the thumb and forefinger at point marked 'X', to keep from unwinding. Now wind the other short end around the other strand for the other same number of turns, but in the opposite direction.

3. This shows how the knot would look if held firmly in place. Actually, as soon as released, the turns equalize.

4. And the turns look like this. Now pull on both ends of the monofilaments.

5. As pulling on the ends is continued, the turns gather as above and draw closer together (at this point the short ends may be worked backward, if desired, to avoid cutting off too much of the material).

6. Appearance of the finished knot. All that remains to be done is to cut off the short ends close to the knot.

If you wish to attach a dropper fly to your line only cut off one end of the line and use the other end to tie on the dropper.

The Single and
Double fisherman's
knot

(This knot is not recommended for a hard nylon line). Place the two pieces of line alongside each other so that they overlap. Take one end (A) and make a half hitch which includes the other piece of line (B). Ensure that (A) points away from you. Repeat this procedure with the other end of the line, so that end (B) points away from end (A).

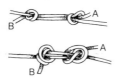

This knot is not reliable for two pieces of nylon. In this case, rather use the double fisherman's knot. Lay the two pieces of line alongside each other. Take end (A) and, pointing it away from you, make two loops over (B). Then push (A) through the double loop and pull the knot tight. Repeat this on the other side. Draw the knots together. Again a dropper can be made with one end of the line. Cut off the ends of the line if they are not required.

Trout Fly knots
The Four-Turn
Water knot

This knot is a complete breakaway from the blood knot and offers the following advantages:

☐ It is stronger (98% of line-breaking strain)

☐ Once mastered, it is quicker and easier to tie

☐ It results in a trailing dropper which is less likely to tangle. Compare the blood knot dropper which sticks out at right angles.

Although primarily of great advantage to the fly-fisherman it has definite uses in other types of angling.

It can only be used where there is one free end in the line which is tucked through the loop. It cannot therefore be used to repair line breaks a long way back from the hook. Practice is needed to perfect tightening up of the knot. If this is done incorrectly—*i.e.* if the knot is allowed to twist, or if all strands are not tightened evenly—the result will be much weakened.

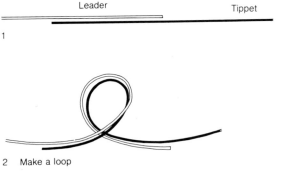

Leader   Tippet

1

2   Make a loop

3   Turn into loop four times

4   Apply plenty of saliva for lubricant and tighten up slowly, ensuring the knot does not twist. Tied properly it is stronger than the blood knot

The Turle knot   Thread the end of the leader downwards through the eye of the (wet) fly and draw the fly well up the leader to be out of the way. Make a running loop with the end of the leader and tighten the knot, but not completely. Pass the fly through the loop and draw the leader tight with the knot on the upper side of the neck of the hook. Take care to keep the wings and fibre of the fly clear of the knot when tightening it.

The Nail knot   This is used to attach the leader to your tapered line when no loop is provided.

Perforate the fly line with a pin. Heat the pin to enlarge the hole and thread the end of the nylon through.

Wind the nylon around the fly line five times. Bring the end back and lay it alongside the line.

Now take the turn of nylon back over itself.

Wind over until all the original turns are used up.

Pull hard on the ends of the nylon, carefully pushing the coils together. Cut off the loose end on the nylon where it enters the fly line, and finally varnish the knot.

Before tightening a knot, apply saliva to lubricate the nylon and prevent friction.

23

The Match-stick knot

This is also used to attach the leader to your tapered line, or backing to your fly line.

1. Use a tapered nail or match-stick. Hold the line, leader and nail/match-stick alongside one another as shown in Figure 1, allowing ample overlap. Wind the leader downward around the match-stick and itself 6 times. Then run the end of the leader back along the match-stick under the loops.

2. Pull both ends of the leader tight. Slip the knot down the match-stick and tighten it by pulling both ends of the leader as you do so. Slip the match-stick out and retighten the knot by once again pulling the leader ends.

3. Finally, pull the line and leader tight and clip the end of the line and leader close to the knot.

For illustration refer to nail knot.

Looking after your tackle

After your day's fishing, check your rod, reel, line and tackle.

Care of your reel

Keep your reel clean and oiled. Wash it in water to clean off all the sand and dirt. An old toothbrush or shaving brush is useful in removing dirt and grease. Dry the reel thoroughly with a clean rag and oil all the movable parts. As oil will run out of the reel, it is preferable to use a lubricant that is heavier than oil, e.g. a light grease made up of two parts of paraffin wax and one part of light lubricating oil. The spool should be removed and cleaned with a cleansing fluid such as carbon tetrachloride which can also be used to clean the reel. Remember that the fumes of carbon tetrachloride are poisonous and are particularly dangerous if inhaled while you smoke.

It is advisable to replace any parts showing signs of hard wear, thus reducing the risk of your reel breaking down when you are away on a fishing trip. You should also check your reel for worn line guides or pick-up arms. A good way of keeping your reel free of dust and dirt when it is not used, is to store it in a dry flour bag that has been washed.

Care of your rod

Check your fishing rod and particularly the rod tip and the rings (eyes) to see if they have worn or are out of alignment as a result of loosening binding. The rough edge of a worn runner or tip is the commonest cause of line breaking.

Also check that there are no loose threads from the end of the binding. The latest P.T.F.E. centred rings enable you to turn the centre of the ring, thus presenting a new unworn section from time to time.

Care of your line

Nylon line needs little care and will not rot even if left wet on your reel for several months. Check the last few feet of your line to ensure that it has not frayed, particularly that part which comes into contact with the tip of the rod as you cast. Many a fish has been lost when a defective line snaps. Discard any section of the line with a nick or which is kinked after a bad tangle. In fact, it is advisable to cut off the last few feet of line after two or three outings or after catching a large fish. Also, reverse the line on your reel so that it wears evenly and has a longer life. Try to avoid having any knots in your line. Not only does the knot weaken your line but it also catches the remaining line, with the result that the length of your cast is reduced and your line may become entangled. Nylon line will last longer and wear better if, before it is stored, it is dried and given a very thin coating of glycerine. Do not leave your line in strong sunlight for long periods as the suns's rays will oxidize your line, making it stiff and brittle. This will weaken the line, make it harder to handle and shorten its life.

General tackle

A tackle box is useful. The following items should form part of every angler's tackle box: long-nosed pliers, screwdrivers, knife, file, small adjustable spanner, reel, oil, spare line, hooks, sinkers and lures, floats, cotton, split shot, wire trace, a bottle of mercurochrome for wounds and a box of plasters.

The angler who does not check his tackle box from one fishing trip to the next, will invariably find that he is short of tackle or that what is there is not in good condition. An angler should also have a landing net, keep net and, for certain types of fishing, a gaff.

Casting
Using an open-face or fixed-spool reel

Hold the reel (which is attached to your rod) between the second and third fingers of your hand. If your rod has a long handle you may hold the butt of the rod with your hand. Click back the pick-up of the reel and support the line with your index finger. Before you start your casting movement, note a point in the water where you wish to drop your bait. Facing that mark, take the rod back over your head to the one o'clock position, the butt pointing towards your mark. Your wrist should go back with the rod. Timing is very important. While the weight of the lure or sinker is still pulling the rod tip back, start the forward casting movement by quickly bringing the butt of the rod towards your body and at the same time straightening your right arm. The precise moment to straighten your index finger and so release the line is only discovered by practice, but you should soon be able to cast within a few centimetres of your mark. If your lure or sinker flies almost straight up into the air instead of travelling out some distance, you are releasing the line too soon. A trajectory of 45° at the commencement of the cast achieves the furthest distance.

You may also cast by bringing the rod back sideways, as far back as your arm comfortably reaches. Swing the rod forward to gain momentum and release the line when the rod is approximately halfway between the back position and the point you are facing.

For distance and accuracy, the length of the line from the end of the rod to the sinker should not be more than half a metre. If it is longer, you will not have full control but tend to hook into obstacles behind you. If you wish to cast particularly far, you will have to use a heavier sinker, but then the casting action may cause the weight of the sinker to snap a light line or damage an unsuitable rod. To prevent this, tie a leader of approximately 4,5 m of heavier line to the end of your line and attach your heavier sinker to this. Do not overload your reel with line. If you do this, several coils may come off the reel at once, causing a tangle. Too little line, however, reduces the casting performance.

Using a centre-pin reel

Unclip the drum, hold it lightly with your thumb resting on the line as it comes off the reel before passing through the runners. Execute the cast and when the rod is more or less in the 11 o'clock position, release your thumb from the line. The actual moment of release depends to a large extent on the size of the bait and the flexibility of the rod.

Some centre-pin reels have a spindle attached to the backing plate, on to which one can slip the drum to facilitate two-handed casting which affords not only the ease of casting of a fixed-spool reel but also all the advantages of the centre-pin reel in playing a fish.

Remember that the secret of all good casting lies in moving your body with your arm.

Weather effects and water conditions

The weather determines the state of the fish's home, its food supply, its breeding habits – in fact, its very existence. Fish are accordingly very sensitive to any change in the weather. They are able to detect the smallest variations in temperature and will react accordingly, depending for the most part upon the type of fish and the temperature trend during that season. A steady temperature rise in spring causes coarse fish to spawn, whereas certain types of fish, such as barbel and bream, remain in a state of hibernation during the cold months. In winter a drop in temperature will cause fish to go off the bite and proceed to the warmest place, usually deep water, whilst in summer a drop in temperature usually has an invigorating effect, bringing fish into the shallows. During summer when the water is warm, a rise in temperature may cause fish to seek comfort in the cold deeper water or in the rapids of a river where the water is more highly oxygenated. Similarly, in time of drought, fish will seek cool and well aerated waters, whereas in time of flood they will seek the slowest moving water. Floodwaters wash away water weeds and food becomes scarce. Thus, when the water settles, the fish will be on the bite. During a drought, dams and slow-moving sections of the river become overgrown with weed in which innumerable water insects breed, supplying the fish with plenty of food. During these periods the fishing is generally poor. When the water becomes discoloured after rain, fish come looking for food. Fish can thus be attracted to a fishing spot (preferably an inlet to a river or dam) by pouring muddy water into the water or by raking the bottom.

One should also study the water currents. These carry food into certain areas where the fish will follow.

Fishing is generally better on a windy day. The wind starts a movement in the water which loosens the vegetation and dislodges the insects in the vegetation and the fish start feeding. If the wind blows in cold air, however, the fish may go into the deeper water.

It is usually better to fish into the wind as the wind moves both food and warmer water towards the bank on which you are fishing.

Barometer

The barometer also plays an important part in the life of the inland angler for it will accurately foretell if he can expect good or bad fishing, and whether the fish will be deep or closer to the surface. When the atmospheric pressure rises fairly rapidly, fish tend to bite well, particularly black bass and trout. High pressure causes a rise in the oxygen content of the water. This makes fish livelier; they move around more and will bite more readily.

Effect of sound and movement
Sound

Fish do not have a sense of hearing but are particularly sensitive to vibrations which are transmitted by means of nerve organs scattered over their body, notably their head and a line running along the side of their body known as the lateral line. Thus the vibration caused by people talking, by an object being thrown into the water, or by somebody walking on the river bank will be felt by the fish which will be scared away from that area. The vibration will be felt much more easily if the river bank is hollow and the water shallow, but if the water is reasonably deep, you may talk and listen to a wireless without fear of disturbing the fish. Leather or metal-studded wading soles alarm fish but they appear unaffected by rubber soles. Small pebbles thrown into the water seem to attract rather than alarm fish.

On more than one occasion, whilst fishing in a river, I found the fish which had been biting well suddenly stopped biting when an onlooker walked along the bank nearby. Almost immediately the footsteps ceased, the fish started to bite again. This pattern repeated itself when the onlooker returned.

Movement

Fish are nearly all short-sighted. While they cannot see for long distances through water, they can easily detect movement in and outside the water.

An angler fishing in deep clear water is easily visible to fish owing to the refraction of light, and they will be frightened away by much movement. In shallow water, however, the angler will not be seen as easily. Certain fish, such as trout, have very sharp eyesight and will detect movement a long way away. If the sun is directly behind the angler, his shadow on the water's surface in front of him will tend to scare fish. It is, therefore, advisable to face the sun. You should also wear sombre-hued clothing which is less easily detectable and blend in with the surroundings. Avoid white or brightly coloured clothes which are easily perceived by fish.

Smell and taste

Fish have a highly developed sense of smell and taste and this has often led to one angler having better results than another. Once, two boat anglers using the same tackle and bait found that one was catching one fish after the other whilst the other didn't have a bite. The unsuccessful angler eventually discovered he had a trace of petrol on his hands. Once his hands had been washed, he started to catch fish. It is a good rule to wash your hands in the water you are fishing in to neutralise any unnatural smell, as fish will reject a bait because of the human smell on it. For this reason, handle a bait or a lure as little as possible. I have caught a carp which was blind and could only have found the bait

27

by smell. A scent or flavouring may be added to a bait to attract fish, but too much flavouring on paste bait is likely to repel rather than attract fish. The smell of nicotine appears to be particularly repulsive to fish.

Pain

A frequent question is whether fish feel pain. It is apparent that they do, but because they have a less complex nervous system than more developed creatures, they feel pain to a far lesser extent and you would have to imbed the hook in a nerve before a fish really feels pain.

Mucus coating

All fish have a protective covering of mucus or slime. Before he returns a fish to the water, an angler should wet his hands before touching the fish to prevent removing the mucus. If not, the fish may die from fungal infection.

How to strike, play and land a fish
Detecting a bite and the use of an indicator (policeman)

Until you have learned to feel a bite when the line is held over your finger, or if you do not wish to hold your rod, place it in a rod rest or forked stick, and press a small piece of bread, pap or similar substance (the policeman or indicator) on to your line about 0,6 to 0,9 m from the tip of your rod. The rod rest should not be more than 0,31 m high, else the breeze will cause the indicator to swing, making it more difficult to detect a bite. On a windy day, move the rod rest away from the water so that the indicator hangs just off the ground where there is less wind interference. Alternatively, the rod rest may be placed in the water with the indicator hanging 2,5 to 5 cm above the water. About 15 to 25 cm of slack should be left in the line from the tip of the rod to the point where the line enters the water. Never leave too much slack in the line, as the fish must pull all the slack out before you can detect a bite. When a fish bites, the policeman will bob up and down, and when the fish runs with the bait, the line will be pulled straight and the policeman should fall off.

Silver paper makes an excellent policeman for night fishing. You can also make an indicator with a ping-pong ball. Cut a small hole into the ball, insert a hairpin and glue it to the ball to serve as a line clip. Cut a larger hole at the other end of the ball and insert and glue in a light bulb. Solder wires to the bulb and connect them to a battery. This can then be clipped on to the line.

A useful bite detector designed for night fishing and particularly suitable for carp can also be made as shown (see pages 29 & 44).

Until the buzzer sounds to indicate there is a bite, you are free to do something else. Keep an eye on your rod however, as many a rod has been dragged into the water and lost when a large enough fish has taken the bait and swum off.

An angler can sit for hours on end without a bite. This is when the sport can become tedious. But, with the first quiver of the indicator or float, signifying the beginning of a bite, all enthusiasm returns.

Bites vary tremendously according to the type of fish. Even the way in which the same species of fish in the same waters will take the bait will vary according to the conditions of the water, i.e. the depth and temperature, the current, the colour, the amount

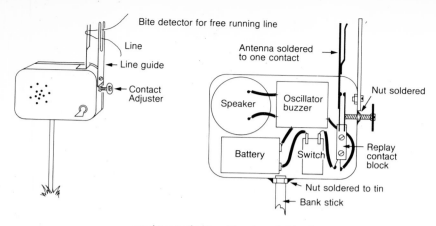

Bite detector for free running line

Line

Line guide

Contact Adjuster

Antenna soldered to one contact

Nut soldered

Speaker

Oscillator buzzer

Battery

Switch

Replay contact block

Nut soldered to tin

Bank stick

and type of natural food available, the temperature above the surface, the weather and the type of bait. A bite does not necessarily mean a fish in the keep net, as usually the fish must be struck. With the exception of yellow-fish, it happens infrequently that a fish hooks itself when it takes the bait. Thus the angler must know how the fish bites in order to know when to strike it. Some bites are very difficult to strike; some must not be struck; some the angler does not need to strike, and others need the strike of experience. They are soon learned. You must also learn to identify the bite of a crab, which will grasp the bait in its claws and slowly move around with it.

In well-fished spots, the fish may become 'educated' and remove the beginner's bait without his knowing it. This will usually only happen, however, if your piece of bait is too large for the fish to take and run off with. Often an angler using a large paste bait may detect a bite and then see the line going slack. The explanation is that the fish becomes aware of the tension on the line and then continuously pushes the bait towards the rod until it breaks into sufficiently small pieces for it to take. Or, a fish may pick up the bait and swim towards you with it. This is when you should take in the slack line and strike.

Float fishing

Fishing with a float is a method at least as old as Isaac Walton's 'Compleat Angler'. It is very popular with European anglers,

Typical floats

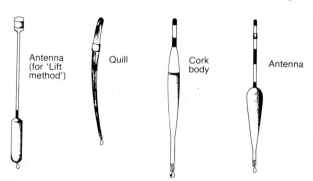

Antenna (for 'Lift method')

Quill

Cork body

Antenna

but for some unknown reason has been largely neglected by anglers in Southern Africa. Since the method can be extremely deadly under most conditions it is well worth using.

The various 'rigs' with which a float can be used can be basically divided into four groups: float ledgering, trotting, the lift method and slow sink.

Float ledgering

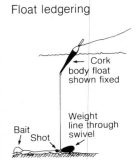

Cork body float shown fixed

Weight line through swivel

Bait
Shot

The point at which the float is set on the line should be about 15 cm more than the depth of the water where you are fishing, so that the hook lies on the bottom. The line is loaded with enough split shot to cock the float and the split shot is clamped on to the line at a point where it will not lie on the bottom. Fish browsing for natural food along the bed of the dam or river will see the bait and pick it up. Bites are usually indicated by the float gently sliding under the surface of the water.

If you wish to cast longer distances and thus need more weight to do so, you may use the 'sliding ledger float' rig. Thread the line through the float ring and then through the weight. The best weights are barrel-shaped sinkers with a swivel at one end. The line is threaded through the swivel eye. Fix a large split shot for a 'stop' below the sinker, and fix another 'stop' above the float at a distance as far from the bottom split shot as the depth of the water. You can also whip on a nylon stop or use a float rubber ring as a stop. The hook should be tied directly to the line about 35 cm below the split shot.

The best floats for 'float ledgering' are either cork-bodied floats tapering to a thin antenna or a large porcupine quill float.

Trotting

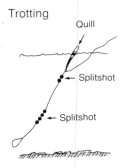

Quill

Splitshot

Splitshot

This is the term used to describe the action when the float is carried along by the current and is so set that the bait trips along the bottom or a few centimetres above it. The float should be allowed to drift along the particular stretch of water, retrieved and cast out to drift down again. By raising the rod as the float goes by, you can avoid slack line and maintain constant contact. This method is particularly effective when you fish for yellow-fish.

The float may either be attached to the line in the normal way, by passing the line through the float cap which will be uppermost, and then through the float ring, or, to detect the more sensitive bites, you may pass a loop through the float ring over the top of the float and tighten the loop.

The float should be accurately set to the required depth by temporarily adding enough weight to the hook to make the float sink. The rig is cast out and the correct depth can be set by adjusting the float up or down the line. For bottom-tripping you would set the float to stand up clearly in the water. If it sinks you have set it too shallow, and if it lies flat you have set it too deep. The split shot should be spread out over about 20 cm, approximately 40 cm away from the hook. There should be enough shot to cock the float so that only 40 per cent of it is visible. The float will indicate bites by 'bobbing', by heeling over and by short runs. The time to strike is either when the float slides under, or when it stops after a run, or if it moves against the current. The float so set is very sensitive and will indicate every movement. Medium-sized porcupine quills are ideal for this method.

The lift method

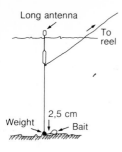

Long antenna

To reel

2,5 cm

Weight

Bait

This method was developed by the Taylor brothers in the United Kingdom. It is the deadliest of all bite detection systems, but is limited in that it works best in calm or almost still water.

The best type of float to use is one with a long antenna. The float should measure 30 cm from tip to ring. Use a very large split shot or a small pierced bullet as a weight. This should be just heavy enough to sink the float and should be attached to the line 5 cm above the hook. I have found a size 8 extra short-shank hook the most effective. Cast out and set the float so that only 5 cm of the antenna is showing. Take up all slack line and get set for action. On picking up the bait, a fish, which usually stands on its head to do so, will also pick up the weight. This will not scare it because the float at the same time lifts the weight. You will see the float lift up in the water. In fact, it may be lifted so far that it rolls over and lies on the surface. Since the float can only move upward when the fish has the bait in its mouth, you may strike with near certainty that you will hook it. You must ignore all sideways float movement since these are caused by fish brushing against the line. This superb technique works with all bottom-feeding fish and is the only really effective method for catching mud-fish.

Slow sink

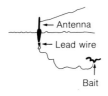

Antenna

Lead wire

Bait

In this method, which is designed for fish feeding near the surface, one simply attaches the float one metre or more from the hook, depending on the depth at which the fish are feeding.

No weights are fixed to the line. It does help, however, to bind some soft lead wire around the float stem near the eye to make the float 'self-cocking'. This can help you to cast out the bait which will sink naturally. Bites will be indicated by the float running across the surface. Small quill floats are best for this method.

Float fishing has great appeal, not only because it is exciting to watch a float, but because it is a very effective way of catching fish. There are no large weights to be easily caught up, and the 'rigs' are simple to make up. By altering the positions of the split shot and varying the sizes of the floats, you may cope with almost any river or still-water conditions.

Striking a fish

Many an angler will try to strike the fish the moment his line moves. This is incorrect and is bad fishing. As a general rule, never be in a hurry to strike immediately you feel a bite or see your indicator move, as a strike before the fish has taken the bait into its mouth will only result in it being lost. You must allow the fish to play with the bait until it takes it properly. When your indicator starts to bob up and down, it is not an indication to strike, only that a fish is biting. When, however, your indicator rises in one continuous movement, either fast or slow, in the direction of the water, it means that the fish has the bait in its mouth. Pick up your rod gently, hold it in an upright position, wind in the slack and strike. I have seen an angler strike a fish with such force that his line broke under the strain. This is uncalled for and should never happen.

As most species of fish have a soft mouth, a violent strike or an attempt to haul the fish in may result in the hook being pulled out of or through the fish's mouth. All that is necessary to set the hook is a backward jerk of the wrist. This is the stage when the fish starts to run to the other end of the dam and the beginner becomes so excited that he tries to pull the fish right on to the bank. Many a fish is lost this way. You must remain calm and play the fish. Hold the rod upright for a second or two to ensure the hook is secure in the fish's mouth and keep the line taut. The fish cannot spit the bait out unless the line is slack. You should now be able to feel the movement of the fish on your line. If the fish runs, loosen your drag slightly (it should be properly adjusted before you start fishing), and let it run. When it stops running and the line becomes slack, wind in the slack immediately, else the fish may tangle your line around an obstruction. Keep your line taut whilst you play the fish or it may throw the hook. You should never give a fish slack line. This is all there is to playing a fish. Never try to wind a fixed spool whilst a fish is running with the line, as this causes the line to twist.

Playing the fish

To begin with, when playing the fish, the inexperienced angler should hold the rod upright and watch the tip of the rod. When the rod tip bends the fish is pulling. Obviously you can feel this as well. Stop reeling and let the fish pull the line against the drag and let it run. Start to reel in again as the tip straightens. A large fish is also played by lifting the rod when it has stopped running, and winding in a metre or two of line at a time as the rod is lowered. Keep the line taut throughout and hold the rod up to absorb the strain of any sudden run or plunge. Try to keep the fish in clear water, away from reeds and other obstructions. If the fish swims towards an obstruction, walk away, keeping the tip of the rod pointed away from the obstruction. The fish will swim in the direction in which the tip of your rod is pointing. If you cannot walk away, head the fish away from the obstruction by applying side strain, i.e. move the tip of your rod sideways, pointing away from the obstruction. Always keep your line taut. The fish will bore, usually downwards, but skill will tell and the fish will soon be brought to the surface — the first sign of its impending defeat. Once the fish is tired, try to lift its head above the surface of the water by holding your rod high. The fish cannot stay with its head out of the water too long and will tire much more quickly. If you allow the fish to keep its head under water, it can see where it is going and fights much more strongly. If, after you have struck the fish, the tip of your rod does not bend, do not wind in your bait but leave it there as the fish will often follow the bait and take it again. It does happen, however, that a fish (and it can be a big yellow-fish or carp) bites very cautiously or even leaves the bait if it feels resistance. If you suspect that this is happening, it may be necessary to strike immediately the fish bites.

Landing the fish

A fish which has been properly played will be so tired that it lies motionless on its side on the surface of the water. Don't assume the battle is over when you have managed to bring the fish into shallow water. When it sees you it will take fright and usually try to run again, particularly if it is a large fish. You should let it do so, as you are more likely to lose it by trying to prevent its last desperate run.

When you have played the fish until it is tired and brought it into

Ruth Babich assisted by her son Michael landing a 14,5 kg Mirror Carp at the Vaal River

the shallows again, do not try to lift it out of the water with your rod. If you hold your rod upright and do not give it any slack, the fish will not get away in the time it takes you to use your landing net. Make sure your landing net is set up and at hand before you start fishing. For an angler using light tackle, the landing net is the most important part of his kit as he cannot lift a heavy fish out of the water without it. Most fish are lost when the excited angler tries to lift them out of the water with his rod instead of using his landing net. Always ensure that you are in a position to use your landing net. It is most frustrating to lose your fish after you have carefully played and brought it in.

If somebody wades into the water to help you to land the fish, he must stand still holding the landing net in the water in front of him whilst you bring the fish towards the net. Many experienced anglers do not use their landing net correctly. Without frightening the fish, it must be carefully placed in the spot to which you wish to bring the fish. When the fish swims over the net, lift the net up and take the netted fish out of the water. Do not try to scoop the fish out of the water as the fish will move away when it sees the net coming towards it. Many a large fish has been lost by an angler trying to scoop it out of the water. The net knocking against the taut line may dislodge the hook from the fish's mouth, and the fish will fall back into the water if it is not yet in the landing net. A very large fish should not be netted tail first as it will usually jump out of the net immediately it feels it. Keep the line taut in the direction of the fish's body so that the net will not dislodge the hook, and bring the net over the fish's head. Once the fish is in your landing net, carry it on to dry land and place it in your keep net. Never try to put the fish into your keep net whilst you are still in the water. Fish are slippery when wet and can easily squirm out of your hands and fall back into the water whilst you are taking the hook out or putting them into your keep net.

Boat fishing

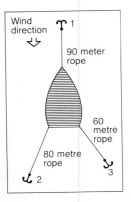

Wind direction

90 meter rope

60 metre rope

80 metre rope

1

2

3

Fishing is easier for the boat angler for he can select his spots and avoid the crowd on the banks. Nor does he have to cast very far.

The anchoring layout illustrated here is recommended. Drop anchor no. 1 and allow the boat to swing down-wind, taking care not to foul the propellers. Allow all the rope out and ensure the first anchor is holding before dropping anchor no. 2. Take the boat to no. 3 position and drop the third anchor. Cut the motors and pull on no. 1 rope until rope no. 3 is taut, and the ropes form the angles as in the sketch. Pull in all the slack and tie the ropes with quick-release knots in case you have to follow a big fish. When anchored, fish with your back to the anchor, and when playing a fish keep the fish away from your back so that it cannot swim round the anchor rope. A hooked fish will often head straight for and under the boat and you will have to swing your rod round quickly, to the end of the boat to avoid the rod or line being broken.

If, after you have brought the fish close to the boat, it still shows a little too much fight to net it safely, you must allow it to swim away again and play it until it is tired, keeping your line taut all the time. If you are on land, you can make the fish swim around in circles and tire it completely by holding the rod at arm's length and making a figure-of-eight movement for a few minutes. Do not try this method from a boat, however, as the fish may swim under the boat. The fish may also be made to swim and thus tired out by the angler holding the rod upright and walking up and down the river bank or side of the dam, although this could cause you to lose a large fish. The fish will swim in the direction in which the angler walks.

No angler should fish without a lifejacket from a boat or canoe, however safe it may seem. Sudden gusts of wind or a storm can make the water very choppy and I have seen many a boat capsized. By law you are obliged to wear a lifejacket when in a boat. Accidents do happen, and an angler well clad in a jersey, extra socks and gum-boots will stand no chance if the boat should capsize or if he should overbalance and fall out.

Remember that fish sense vibration and that a boat acts as an echo chamber. Therefore, you must be very quiet when in a boat. It is advisable to wear soft-soled shoes. You should also remain seated, as it is not only much safer, but fish will be frightened away by the movement of someone standing up in a boat.

In conclusion, a word of advice. Do not set out to fish with the object of catching more fish than the next angler. Fish purely for your own satisfaction. The greedy fisherman is never a good or a true angler.

3 Carp

(Cyprinus carpio)

Three types are found in South Africa: full-scale or King carp (completely covered with scales, as their name suggests); leather carp (almost naked of scales and with a thick soft leather-like skin), and mirror carp, the most common variety, so named because they have three or four rows of very large scales running along each side of their bodies.
Leather and mirror carp are descended from full-scale carp and will revert to the full-scaled variety in later generations.

The early settlers in South Africa found that the rivers had few indigenous freshwater fish. Carp was one of the first sporting fish to be introduced to the Cape of Good Hope, and they prospered exceptionally well: South African waters are very fertile and the carp have a high growth rate. Some anglers feel that carp have prospered too well as they are found in most rivers and dams throughout the country today. At any rate, they comprise the bulk of fish caught inland, provide good sport and, if cooked properly, are well worth eating.

Feeding habits

Large carp are very wary feeders and are generally suspicious and cautious, with the result that they are not usually caught in easily accessible places. Carp are bottom feeders, preferring muddy spots where they can feed on rotten vegetation, insects, blood-worms and worms. They feed by standing on their heads.

Carp can be caught throughout the year as they are able to tolerate a wide range of temperatures. There are peak periods when they will be more readily caught. In fact, contrary to common belief, depending on the water conditions and intensity of the rate of feeding, carp angling can be so hectic that the angler is able to use only one rod. Carp are particularly active when the water temperature is 64° F. The best fishing is invariably to be had at this temperature when the wind (other than an east wind) has been blowing and carp are feeding well. An east wind normally means bad weather is on its way: the barometric pressure drops and fish of all types, not only carp, will sound. In summer, carp may be caught right through the day and night. In winter, carp will feed more freely during the day, and as the smaller carp do not usually feed once the water temperature drops below 58°F, one is likely to catch the larger specimens which can weigh up to 30 kg.

The best average depth for carp fishing is approximately 3,5 m, except in midwinter when the water becomes very cold. Carp will move into deep water in the thermocline where the temperature remains fairly constant. The larger carp will not bite on a bright moonlight night and the best night fishing is to be had on a dark night.

Breeding habits

Carp breed in summer. When the water temperature rises above 60°F, carp in either a river or dam start to spawn on aquatic vegetation recently covered by water. In a dam therefore, carp will only spawn on a rising water level *i.e.* after the first rains. A carp is most likely to take a spinner when it is spawning. In fact, any sizeable freshwater fish will at certain times and under certain conditions take an artificial lure.

Each female spawns a number of times a season and will produce anything from 300 000 to 900 000 eggs, depending on her size. After the eggs have been laid they are left unguarded by the parents. Only about one per cent of the fry reach maturity: many die or are eaten by other fish, particularly barbel. River carp migrate when they breed and will swim upstream seeking quiet tributaries and shallow backwaters. Carp grow very rapidly if the feeding conditions are right. It is recorded that a 3-year-old fish has attained a weight of 14 kg. Carp live for many years. Some specimens have been known to survive for more than 80 years. They are particularly intelligent and in captivity can even be trained to take bread from a person's fingers. Scientists have likened their intelligence to that of a chicken.

Choosing a likely spot

Before you start fishing, use a stick to test the condition and nature of the river or dam bottom at the spot where you wish to fish. If the bottom is rocky, e.g. a river-bed, you should try variations in the the position of your hook and sinker. You can try using 1 or 2 hooks with no sinker – in which case the weight of the bait alone is used to cast out – or a running sinker, swivel and 2 hooks. Your bait will lie on the bottom. Vary the length of each trace. If the bottom is muddy, tie a fixed sinker onto your line and tie the first trace about 30 cm above the sinker and the second about 30 cm above that, so that the bait is lifted out of the mud, where the fish can find it. The purpose of using different rigs is to find out how the fish are feeding at that spot. The golden rule for carp fishing is to use as little tackle as possible.

Carp fishing can be a waiting game, so two rods may be used, with a running sinker fitted to the one line and a fixed sinker to the other. The rods should be placed on rod rests in such a way that there is no appreciable angle between the rod tip and the line, so that it may be pulled out without resistance. Ensure that the line is not caught in the groove of the rest but can run off easily. One should use the rest rather than hold the rod, when movement is imparted to the bait, which causes any self-respecting carp to flee for its life.

Never start fishing by tying the sinker and length of trace in the same manner. You should also vary the flavouring of your bait and use a different bait on each hook until you have discovered how the fish are biting and which type of bait they prefer that particular day. Remember which bait is on which hook and change to the bait which the fish favour. Finding the right bait is to a large extent a matter of trial and error until you have learned the characteristics of a particular dam.

If after a while you find you are unsuccessful, bring in the line fitted with the running sinker, and attach a small unpainted float onto the trace just above the hook so that the bait will be lifted off the ground. If this does not bring results, try fishing without a sinker. Remember to keep to the right depth of water.

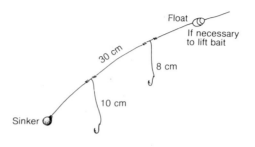

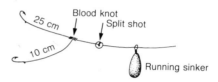

If you are fishing in an area where there is water grass, use a bait that will float. If you mix rice crispies into your conventional porridge bait, it will float for about 20 minutes. You can also try cutting a piece of stale bread into cubes which are fitted into a hook and cast without a sinker. The bread cube will float and as it absorbs water it will slowly sink to the bottom. As it sinks it will often be picked up by a carp.

I recall once throwing small crusts of bread onto the water and watching carp readily taking them. When I put a hook into a piece of crust and threw it out, a carp started to play with it. It even pushed it around for a while but was reluctant to take it. It could obviously sense the hook. If you strike and miss a good bite, you should move off to another spot, as the fish will not take the bait at the same spot for some while.

Normally an easily accessible place is not a good fishing spot. Try to choose an inlet (not necessarily a river) into a dam where food will be washed in, or beneath trees where the fish will lie in wait to feed on bird droppings or fallen caterpillars, or near a clump of reeds or weeds where fish will find insects and other forms of food as well as shelter. Water-lilies provide good feeding for nearly every species of fish and, all other things being equal, fishing near lilies is usually good practice.

Look out for Coot – they usually indicate an underwater feeding spot.

The general rule of fishing into the wind also applies to carp, particularly in winter when the sun warms the surface area of the water and fish will move to this area which is on the windward side of the dam.

Rod	Select a hollow glass-fibre one-piece rod 3 m long with a test curve of 0,68 kg. A line with a breaking strain of 2,6 kg is best suited to this test curve.

Rod

Select a hollow glass-fibre one-piece rod 3 m long with a test curve of 0,68 kg. A line with a breaking strain of 2,6 kg is best suited to this test curve.

Reel

Use a centre-pin type with a diameter of 7 to 10 cm, which has a greater line capacity.

Hooks

A size 5 short-shank hook and no. 10 open-bend hook are the most suitable.

Length of trace

This depends on the type of method to be used. When you use a fixed sinker, the trace should be 15 to 20 cm long. You should use 2 hooks, the first of which should be tied so that it rests just off the bottom, to have a long trace. The other should be tied so that the bait is some 60 to 80 cm off the bottom. If you find you are catching fish mainly on the top hook you can easily shorten the trace on the bottom hook and increase your chances of catching fish on both hooks.

When you use a running sinker, one trace should be about 25 cm long and the other about 30 cm long. They should never be the same length, or else the two pieces of bait will lie next to each other and become entangled. When a running sinker is used, a fish can pick up the bait without feeling the weight of the sinker, which will not be dragged along the bottom.

When fishing in a fast-moving river, use only one hook and make your trace a little longer so that the bait is free to move around, as fish will be attracted by the movement.

If you find the fish are biting but not taking the bait properly, the reason is probably that the fish are feeding where the bait lies without picking it up. To overcome this, halve the length of your trace.

Sinker

The smaller carp – up to some 1,4 kg – will take your bait regardless of the weight of the sinker. Larger carp, however, will invariably drop the bait as soon as they feel resistance, so you should try to use as light a sinker as possible. A sinker of 14 gm is ideal but naturally, the heavier your line the heavier the sinker will have to be.

If the bottom of the river is sandy or rocky and you wish to try fishing without a sinker, but you cannot cast far enough using only the bait as weight, tie a swivel on to your line in place of the fixed sinker and roll a ball of clay or mud on to the swivel. The clay will give you sufficient weight to cast but will dissolve once it is in the water, so that you will be able to detect the bite much more easily. The same result can also be achieved by wrapping a stone or gravel in tissue paper. Tie the paper on to your line with a length of cotton. When the paper dissolves in the water the stone or gravel will fall out.

Bait

A carp usually prefers a paste bait or maize pips to insects or worms. After it has rained in summer, carp will readily take earthworms. For the best effect, however, you should use a very small hook (no. 10 open-bend). The earthworm is carefully

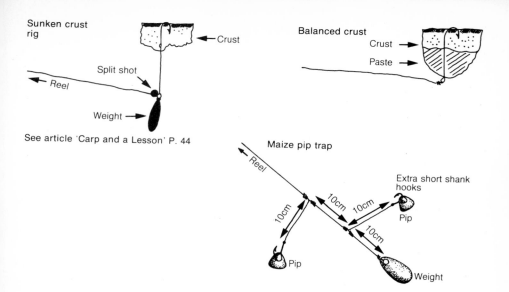

Sunken crust rig

Crust

Split shot

Reel

Weight

See article 'Carp and a Lesson' P. 44

Balanced crust

Crust

Paste

Maize pip trap

Reel

Extra short shank hooks

10cm

10cm

10cm

Pip

10cm

Pip

Weight

hooked through its collar so that it stays alive and both ends wriggle. If catfish should become a nuisance, cover the worm with a soft porridge bait shaped to the size of a small banana. The small fish will invariably be attracted to it. While the big fish look on, the small fish will break up the porridge bait. Eventually the large fish will take the worm. Large carp are often caught on worm.

The usual paste bait is made from a handful of brown or white bread, mixed with milk and water and well kneaded, or from a maize meal mixture. An essence or a flavouring, such as curry powder, aniseed, custard or other flavoured powder, is a most effective additive.

Another effective method is to roll the bait in oats or bran. As the bait sinks the food particles will fall off the bait leaving a trail on which fish of all kinds will home in. The size, texture and hardness of your bait determines to a large extent the size carp you will catch. One may legally ground bait by using a very large soft paste bait that disintegrates in the water.

With experience, you may practise selective carp angling. A large bait will give a large fish more time and opportunity to chase away smaller fish before the bait is broken up. If you are plagued by smaller carp, harden your bait to prevent it being broken up.

When you use 2 hooks, put a large bait as an attractor bait on the hook, and a small pea-sized bait on the other. Whilst the smaller fish play with the big bait, a large fish will often take the small bait.

The size of the bait you should use depends on the type of water you are fishing and on factors which will influence fish in that stretch of water, such as ground-baiting. You should, therefore, vary the size and type of your bait until you establish what the fish will take.

Each dam has its own characteristics and the type of flavouring you should use varies from dam to dam. For example, carp in the

A 8,5 kg Full-Scale Carp caught below the barrage on Vaal River by Michael Babich on 1,8 kg breaking strain line using a Fresh-water Shrimp as bait

Vaal Dam have a preference for custard, while those in Settler's Dam have a preference for aniseed. These preferences only last for 2 to 3 years when the fish become wise to the situation.

The colour of the bait is immaterial, except in the pattern of light reflected from it, as carp are colour-blind. Good results have been achieved, however, by colouring the bait yellow.

If you find that after a period of good fishing small fish suddenly come on the bite, change the size and texture of your bait. Also try adding an astringent liquid such as Dettol, methylated spirits or T.C.P. to your bait. The younger fish have a sharper sense of smell/taste than the mature fish, and these substances are normally unacceptable to the small fish.

Very good results have also been achieved by allowing a paste bait to ferment. The bait will ferment if it is left in a plastic bag for a few days.

Some useful bait recipes
Porridge

Take 2¾ cups maize meal and ¼ cup flour and mix dry. Boil 3 cups of water and add the mixture and the required flavouring. Cook for 5 - 10 minutes while stirring with a wooden spoon or stick. Remove the lid of the pot and allow the mixture to cool. Knead well and roll the bait into a ball. Do not place it in a plastic bag as it will sweat and become soft. The flour to meal ratio may be altered, or custard added, but the solid content should be equal to the amount of water used.

Bread	Brown or white bread kneaded into a smooth soft paste, with the water being fished, is a commonly used and effective bait. Both types of bait should be mixed with honey, an essence, butter or a similar substance to prevent it from hardening, particularly in cold water.

Better results are obtained if you use the water where you fish to make your bait. A single maize pip boiled until it is soft is also a very effective bait in most waters.

Remember there is no infallible bait and fish are notoriously inconsistent in their feeding habits. At times, carp will become totally preoccupied with certain natural foods and will not easily take a bait.

Recipes

In several countries carp are looked upon as a delicacy, and they have been commercially farmed for centuries. There is an art in preparing carp for the table, however. Carp should never be cooked fresh but should be put into the deep freeze for a week or two.

French recipe

Clean and skin a 2-kg carp, cutting off the head, tail and fins. If the fish has roe, carefully remove it, preserving the encasing membrane.

Put the fish in an aluminimum-covered pot and almost cover it with water. Add a heaped teaspoon of 'all spice', a few bay-leaves, a teaspoonful of salt, a little black pepper, a few cloves, a sliced onion, the rind of half an orange and half a lemon.

Boil on high for 15 minutes and then add 2 wine glasses of sherry and simmer for another 15 minutes.

The sauce

To be cooked and stirred constantly at medium heat.

To one cup of thick cream, a tablespoon of butter and 2 egg-yolks, add 1 or 2 tablespoons of stock from the pot in which the carp was cooked, season with a dash of salt and paprika and a teaspoonful of mustard. Having removed the membrane, stir the roe of the fish into the sauce. If there is no roe, thicken the sauce with a little flour. The roe sauce is a perfect complement to the fish. Add a glass of sherry.

Czechoslovakian recipe

Fillet and cut into large portions. Season with salt and pepper, roll in flour, dip in beaten egg-yolk, toss in bread-crumbs and deep-fry in hot oil until golden brown.

Alternatively, fillet and cut into portions. Season well and sprinkle with caraway seeds, roast in butter in hot oven basting frequently for an hour or so until golden brown and crispy. Serve with a sweet and sour salad consisting of potatoes, apples, mayonnaise and capers.

Small fish may be minced finely after being filleted and boned, to make fish cakes. Ingredients: 1 raw egg, salt and pepper and thyme. Do not add bread. Fry in shallow oil.

Immigrant anglers have been astonished at the methods we successfully employ to catch carp, which are completely foreign to them. The following article on carp fishing by a newcomer to South Africa from England is included for their benefit.

The stars were winking out one by one as the unseen sun began
to herald the start of the new day. The breeze whispered among
the russet-tipped rushes, softly caressing last seasons weaver
nests. Some of the weavers were still there, no longer garbed in
rich scarlet and black. Mousey like their wives, they were
beginning to twitter their dawn chorus. The raw light of morning
was silver-tipping the crests of the small waves as they rushed
at the shore. The air was crisp and clear.

It was May on the Highveld and the bite of winter was in the air.
We were fishing a private dam quite close to Johannesburg. We
had both been in South Africa for about six months, and like many
another immigrant to this country, were experiencing carp fishing
of a standard unbeatable anywhere in the world. In the United
Kingdom, to catch more than half a dozen 7-kg carp and maybe
one of 10 kg during a *whole* season would have been cause for
celebration. There carp are fewer in number, frequently small and
incredibly difficult to catch. This has resulted in vast studies in
carp lore and techniques of fishing. Men have devoted half their
lives to just such a cause.

Well, there we were, two thoroughly brain-washed English carp
anglers, determined at all costs not to allow any local techniques
to influence our 'infallible' methods. But this day was to teach us
a lesson. You can't ignore the success of methods developed by
an equally keen brotherhood of carp anglers some 10 000 km
from the cold-water carp anglers of Britain. There is something to
be said for both schools of approach. As we sat there hunched
over our rods we were some four hours away from learning just
this.

We had both rigged up two rods each. They were 0,78 kg test
curve specially designed carp rods brought from the U.K. We had
attached Mitchell reels loaded with 3-kg line. We used no
weights, no floats. The hook was blood-knotted direct to the line.
Hooks were size 4 'Model Perfects', sharpened to needle points.
Around each hook were kneaded balls of breadpaste about the
size of a ping-pong ball. The rods were set in two rests in such
a manner that they were pointing directly along and in line with the
line. The bail arms on the reel were left open to allow line to run
freely. The line in turn was threaded through the antenna of a
miniature transistorised bite detector. These detectors register
movement of the 'free-running' line and are not at all like the large
fixed-line detectors commonly used here (see illustration P.29).

For those interested in building such things for themselves,
each detector is built into one of the old 50-gram tobacco tins.
(Any small tin will do). The detector itself is a Post Office type
relay contact, to one side of which is soldered a 'y'-shaped piece
of piano wire. The line is threaded through this 'y'. The contact is
mounted in the tin and a screw mounted in the side of the tin in
such a way that the contact gap can be adjusted by turning the
screw. Also in the tin is a 2 000 cycle/sec transistorised oscillator,
a small speaker, a 9-volt battery and an on/off switch. A small
buzzer could replace the oscillator, but in this case the battery will
run down much faster. Using a buzzer does however mean that
no speaker is needed, which reduces the overall cost of the
detector. By adjusting the screw, the contacts can be set so

sensitively that even a footfall near them will set them off.

We were fishing a large reedy bay which extended some 60 metres out into the dam. We were fishing the sides, approximately two metres from the edge of the reed-beds and 50 metres from the shore. John had cast out to the left whilst I fished the right-hand side of the bay. All four lines had been out about ten minutes when John's alarm 'bleeped'. In a flash he was crouched over the rod, concentrating on the line, willing the fish to pick up the bait and run. Three minutes later the alarm 'bleeped' again and then commenced an intermittent bleep-bleep-bleep as the line began to pour off the reel. He lifted the rod to vertical and slammed in the pick-up in one smooth motion.

The rod arched as the line cut through the water in a shower of fine spray. The carp was moving fast into the open water, the reel was screaming in protest as the rod throbbed in John's hand. This is the stuff carp fishing is made of – excitement, the sheer power of the fish and the skill of a fine angler anticipating and reacting to every move. Even as an observer I find almost as much enjoyment from the action as the angler himself. The big carp was now 100 metres away and 'kiting' to the left in an attempt to get around the weed-bed. This is a very difficult situation to handle: when the fish adopts an incoming angle of approach, it is quite a problem to turn him outward. John was aware of this and rather than risk everything on the fish changing direction itself (which it was unlikely to do) he made the decision to turn it into the reed-bed directly towards him. He laid his rod to the left and applied heavy side-strain. The fish turned right around and headed back into the open water. The gamble had come off. John's magic touch had worked again. The big carp made more powerful runs and ten minutes later enough line had been gained to get the fish back into the bay. The fight had now settled into a pattern of short runs toward the reeds, with John turning it every time with appropriate side-strain. But this fish was by no means beaten yet. Without any warning it suddenly started 'kiting' to the left again and within seconds it was in the reeds. John promptly flicked open the bail, put the rod back in the rest and sat down to wait, his eyes glued to the line.

'Well, the hook must be well in' he said hopefully. 'I'll give it five minutes, then I'll start heaving!'. Two minutes later the line started moving out into the bay. In a flash, John laid the rod to the right and engaged the pick-up. The immediate side-strain forced the fish into the middle of the bay where it commenced a last 20-m dash for the open water. Two minutes later it slid over the big net. I grasped the net mesh and in a flurry of spray the fish was lifted from the water. It was a fully-scaled bronze beauty, fat and heavy with muscle. It weighed 14,4 kg and was in superb condition. John slid it into the big keep net made from two bicycle wheel rims and a large sack. Later, it would be photographed and released. He was extremely excited and visibly shaking from the effort of beating the fish. 'You know something, that's the biggest carp I have ever caught and by a long way too', he said. His previous best was 8,6 kg, caught in England.

The baits were cast out again (they had all been reeled in when the big carp had taken) and we settled down to wait. One hour later, with three fish in the net, the bites stopped. We discussed the situation and concluded that the fish must have stopped feeding in the mud. Since the temperature was unchanged at 63°F we felt there was no reason for the fish to move off.

We decided to try another British method, i.e. sunken crust. This method can be very effective and at times has provided some really exciting fishing. The 'rig' is quite simple to make up. Firstly, we threaded on a barrel-lead (the type with a swivel at one end) by passing the line through the 'eye' of the swivel. We then tied on a size 6 long-shank hook previously sharpened (hooks are never sharp when you buy them) and finally pinched on a split shot 5 cm from the hook. The split shot acts as a stop for the weight. This means that the crust is anchored 5 cm from the bottom just at carp eye-level. If you were fishing over a 'soft' muddy bottom you would have to allow for the weight sinking into the mud by moving the split shot further from the hook. The crust

Bill Steele in action landing a Kurper at Hartebeespoort Dam

is carefully chosen from the loaf. Crust which is too soft or too brittle easily comes away from the hook. You need the brown crust which can be bent without cracking. We cut off squares 3 x 3 cm and approximately 2 cm thick. The hook was passed in through the inner crust, twisted and the point imbedded in the outer crust. In this way the crust stands the shock of casting without flying into pieces. The lines were cast out and reeled up tight in order to pull the crust under the surface. About half a metre of line was then pulled off the reel and a dough 'policeman' kneaded on to the line between the reel and the first rod ring.

Within minutes I was into a small carp of some 2 kg which was netted quite quickly. During this time I noticed another angler coming toward us from the next bay. As I slipped the fish into the net he remarked: 'Hello, I see you are catching a few, I have not had a bite. What are you doing, are you using maize pips?' We said 'No' and proceeded to explain the sunken crust method. He was very interested in everything, but he decided to stay with his maize pip method.

He reckoned the water temperature would begin to rise soon and that when it did the carp would only be interested in small baits. 'That nice yellow colour and that smell will tempt them; you wait and see' he said. To an Englishman his maize pips (sweetcorn as we called it) seemed a most unlikely method, especially when he explained his 'maize pip trap' to us. We humoured him a bit, said 'good luck' and carried on with our sunken crust. He then went back to his chosen pitch, melted into the bankside and carried on with his fishing.

'He can't be serious', John remarked. 'Mind you, apart from his methods, he seems to be very knowledgeable. Says he's been at it for 20 years.' As we settled down to fish, I couldn't help thinking that the friendly fisherman's ideas and logic behind his method were in fact basically sound. Nevertheless, head in sand, I dismissed the whole thing as a local peculiarity and returned my attention to the 'policeman' on my line.

We caught three more small carp in the next half-hour and then everything went dead . . . no more bites! Half an hour later there were still no bites and we began to discuss the problem. We checked the water temperature and noted that it had risen marginally. This was not surprising; the sun had been up some three hours and we were fishing into the breeze. We could expect the warmer water to get pushed up against our bank. John decided to try balanced crust over a nearby weed-bed. He reasoned that the carp may have come up from the bottom to browse on nymphs and other marine life in the weeds. I was not so sure and decided to try float fishing with the 'lift method' and worm as bait.

John's 'balanced crust' is another well proven U.K. method for carp in weedy situations, especially where carpets of grassy weed grow over the bed of a lake or dam. The theory is that the balanced bait will settle on top of the weeds where it is easily seen and picked up by the carp. A bait which sinks is far less likely to be found by the fish. This is a free-running rig consisting only of a sharpened long-shank hook knotted to the line. This hook is embedded in crust and bread paste is moulded around the shank. The amount of paste used should be just enough to counteract the buoyancy of the crust, giving a virtually weightless bait once it is under the surface. The method can be very effective, but on this occasion it was to prove fruitless.

My 'lift method' rig began to show signs of life as the float began to make short slow movements across the surface. On striking, I found myself attached to a small crab which was quickly removed and turned into bait.

Out went the float tackle again and I relaxed – there's nothing quite like watching a big antenna float. The float seems to be imbued with a latent attraction. You are always sure it will move any minute. Well, it did just that a couple of minutes later. It rose up in the water and I struck. A few seconds later I landed a fresh-water turtle. These things really stink and I was pleased to see it drop off the hook and make for the water. After this, I decided to stop float fishing, to sit back and just watch John.

Nothing was happening there either, and I began to watch the birds busying themselves in the reeds. It was not long before I noticed that the fisherman along the bank was bent into a good fish. Ten minutes later he had another and soon after that yet another one.

'Hey John', I said, 'watch this guy along the bank. He is pulling them out non-stop'. John looked at me, looked at the yet again well-bent rod of the angler, and said, 'you don't suppose . . . well, I mean you don't think that corn really works?' There followed some hasty rummaging in tackle boxes. 'I have everything to make up the maize pip trap', said John. 'So have I, but there's a snag . . . no maize pips!' The friendly angler was pleased to give us some. 'Take as many as you want, they are in that tin', he said as he battled with yet another fish. 'And don't forget the distances in the rig are very important; everything is 10 cm away from everything'.

We tied two blood knots into the line, one 15 cm from the end and the other 10 cm further up the line from that. One free end (dropper) from each blood knot was snipped off and to the others we tied extra short-shank size 8 Mustard hooks sharpened as keenly as possible. Finally, we tied on a 30 gram pear-shaped lead weight to the end of the line. By the time the knot was tightened the weight was 10 cm from the first blood knot. A single maize pip was attached to each hook with the hook point just showing.

The principle behind the rig is quite simple. The fish picks up the pip and by virtue of its inertia the lead weight drives the hook home. This was the aspect which we had refused to believe. We felt sure the fish would eject the bait immediately, and the weight therefore would never have the opportunity of driving home the hook. The facts are different. It really works and every time, too. It is similar to the old favourite 'paternoster' except that monofilament makes up the rig instead of the erstwhile brass wire, and the distances are much shorter. The hooks must be very sharp. If you can slide the hook point across your thumb nail (with the hook vertical) then it is *not* sharp.

The way the rod is set up is important. Everything must be tight;

any slack will be disastrous. The reel clutch must be set to slip at about 0,7 kg (the rod test curve), otherwise the line may snap on the strike. The rod is set with the point up and the tip is watched for bites. It must be watched closely; this is the easiest way to lose a rod that I know of. Even a small carp can pull your whole outfit in! As soon as the rod tip moves, your fish is on: the hook is already in, the strike merely drives it home. You must be quick, otherwise the fish will either get off or, more likely, you will be diving after the rod.

The lines were cast out, mine to the point of the reed-bed 60 metres away, John's to the edge of the reeds some 40 metres away.

Almost immediately both rod tips bucked and we were both into fish. John's hook must have been driven into a nerve, for his fish surged right out of the water in a tremendous burst of spray and sizzled across the bay straight into the reeds. It was a good one. 'I'll let it rest until yours is in,' said John. My fish was a small 1 kg mirror scale carp and was quickly landed. Meanwhile, John's fish had not budged. This was not too surprising, as the speed at which it had hit the reeds had carried it well into the jungle. Two minutes later it still had not moved and John began gently to pick up the line with his rod held high. Almost immediately there was a tremendous crashing and splashing deep inside the reed-bed and the line went slack.

'Did you see that?' he asked. 'Big as a pig, would have filled an enormous glass-case'. He was right, it was a big fish. Its dash across the bay had been so fast and so powerful that it was quite unstoppable. However, that is the way it goes with angling. The big U.K. carp dream is a 20 kg fish. This was maybe not that big, but it was certainly a terrific fish. This was the first time John and I had ever seen a carp of such a size and we were very excited.

After that John also fished the point of the weed-bed. If he hit another one like the lost monster he wanted it out in the open.

We continued to catch carp at half-hour intervals: nothing large, but every one a fighter. The maize pip trap was a winning method. Its effectiveness was proven as far as we were concerned. We could not help thinking that this was a method our friends in England could well offer up for experimentation as a day-time strategy. As a result of the friendly angler's advice we were experiencing a red-letter day among the carp, a day we would store in memory for a long time. We continued to catch fish until dusk, and among the fish we landed were several nice yellow-fish and one catfish. The method obviously had applications to other fish too.

We returned our fish to the water and watched them move out from the shallows, leaving little bow waves in the now still surface. 'Some of those will be monsters one day and then we will catch them again', said John. 'You know, my arms ache. I have not had a day's fishing like that for a long time'. We packed up our tackle and headed for the car. The stars were lighting up one by one. A mouse ran across our path and disappeared into his own small grassy jungle. It was the end of a great day – a day of learning, a day of success.

4

Yellow~fish

(the *Barbus* group; family *Cyprinidae*)

The following types are found in South Africa:
Large-mouth *(Kimberleyensis)*, Small-mouth (Holubi),
Paper-mouth *(Mattozzi)*, Lowveld Small-scale *(Polylepsis)*,
Large-scale *(Marequensis)*, and Lowveld Scalie *(Natalensis)*..

Other less common types of yellow-fish are found in the
various rivers and dams and the same type of yellow-fish may
differ in size, appearance and habit in other rivers and dams.

In the large specimens the head is broad and the eyes appear
relatively narrow, hence the colloquial name 'kalwerkop'.

Feeding habits

This fish naturally feeds on live bait and will bite readily on crabs,
crickets, worms, small frogs, baby birds and insects. A
yellow-fish will also take a paste bait and a trout fly in a fast flowing
stretch of river. The yellow-fish is very suspicious: protruding
ends of line near the bait, too heavy a sinker or a sudden
movement on the bank will scare it away. The best results have
been achieved with light sensitive tackle.

Breeding habits

Yellow-fish are found in dams and in rivers where they prefer fast
moving water. Favourite haunts are deep holes and those places
where natural food is plentiful. A most likely spot is just below a
rapid or in an eddy. In dams yellow-fish are lazier and do not grow
as large as those in rivers where both small-mouth and
large-mouth yellow-fish are found. Large-mouth yellow-fish grow
to well over 15 kg in weight whereas the small-mouth species
usually weighs between 4 and 5 kg. Once the river starts to flow
more heavily in spring, the fish make their way upstream in search
of suitable spawning beds. They spawn in clean gravel beds in the
shallow portion of the river and then depart to deeper water. The
eggs hatch after three or five days, depending upon the water
temperature.

Size hook

A small short-shanked hook, size 8 or 10 should be selected as
the fish has a long mouth. Wherever you may use live bait, use a
no. 2 long-shank hook with barbs on the shank to secure the bait.
When putting on the bait, ensure that there are no loose ends to
the line as the bait must look as natural as possible. When using
paste, use a no. 2 short-shank hook. If small-mouth yellow-fish
are biting, change the size of your hook to a no. 4.

Line

When the yellow-fish takes a bait it usually does so with a sudden
long and powerful run. Many a rod and reel have been lost on
yellow-fish because the ratchet was not adjusted properly. Once,
a 1-kg yellow-fish stripped some 25 m of line off my reel during its
first mad run. A heavier line (between 4½ and 5 kg breaking
strain) should be used.

The yellow-fish is one of the finest fighting course fish in the world.

Length of trace

When using a fixed sinker, fish with two traces: the bottom one about 30 cm long and the top one about 20 cm long. If you use a running sinker, tie your trace in the same manner as for carp fishing.

Type of sinker

When fishing in a stream, use a slightly heavier sinker (between 30 and 40 gm), but light enough to allow the current to move the bait. Particularly good results have been obtained by fishing without a sinker in a river and allowing the current to carry the bait downstream. The large yellow-fish are often scared away when they feel the resistance of a sinker. If the current is very strong, however, a sinker or pieces of shot sufficiently heavy to prevent the bait from being lifted to the surface, will have to be placed along the trace. You should use a longer trace, however, so that the current may impart movement to the bait.

Bait

A good paste bait can be made by mixing a raw egg with white flour until the paste is the texture of chewing gum. Adding the body juice of a crab is also helpful. A yellow-fish will take any live bait, particularly a crab which may be found hiding under a stone in the shallows and in irrigation furrows. One usually breaks off the two large pincers but not the legs. The crab may be tied to the hook with a piece of cotton. A hole should also be made in its back so that the juices can run out, as the smell will attract fish.

Yellow-fish have also been caught on bass lures, spinners and flies in streams where the water conditions are right, usually just after rain when the river flows strongly. In winter, when the rivers do not flow, fly fishing will not bring results. Yellow-fish in a dam will seldom take a lure and then usually only at the inlet into the dam. The best results will be obtained by using a lure such as an insect or frog, when insects and flying ants have come out and are falling into the water. The black and white hairy caterpillar which hatches out on the riverside willows, usually in October, is also an excellent bait.

I have had excellent catches of yellow-fish with the following wet trout flies: Silver March Brown, Black and Peacock, the Polystickle and the Muddler Minnow.

On a summer evening, a dry black gnat or sedge-pattern fly is deadly.

I have also caught yellows, usually the larger specimens, on a small dead fish bait, made up as follows:

Cast out the bait and let it lie on the bottom, occasionally giving a twitch to the line. Catfish will also readily take this bait. When the yellow-fish runs with the bait, don't strike it immediately. It will stop and take the fish deeper into its mouth. Strike when it starts its second run.

Float

If the fish are not biting on the bottom, try using a large quill float in a stream, fixing five BB pieces of shot about 30 cm above the hook to keep the bait down. Vary the depth of your bait until you

51

find the depth at which the fish are feeding. Fish feeding at a particular level will tend to ignore a bait outside that level.

How to strike

If the drag is set correctly, the fish will usually strike itself when it grabs and runs with the bait. Let the fish run, but do not give it slack or else you will usually lose it. A yellow-fish is very excitable, panics when it is hooked and exerts itself so much that it is tired after a few minutes, when it can easily be brought in.

Recipe

The yellow-fish is not a good table fish but is renowned as a sporting fish. Yellow-fish can be good eating, however, if cooked in the following manner:

Wash, clean and behead the fish and place it in a dish. Cover the fish with a mixture of one part of vinegar and half a part of water. Add a teaspoon of salt, a dozen peppercorns and insert one bay-leaf and a blade of mace inside each fish. Cover the dish with greased paper and tie the paper down. Bake for half an hour and then take the dish out of the oven. When cool, replace the dish in a hot oven and leave overnight. The vinegar dissolves the small bones and the fish cooked thus is excellent.

Silverfish

The habits of silverfish are similar to those of yellow-fish and the same method of fishing should be followed. The only variation is in the hook which should be a short-shank not larger than a no. 2.

Silverfish are not as good a sporting fish as yellow-fish and the angler will soon be able to tell whether he has hooked a yellow-fish or a silverfish, as the latter submits much more easily. Silverfish also panic when they are hooked and their frantic run soon exhausts them.

The young silverfish feed readily and will take practically any bait. The young are known as 'paper-mouths' because of their almost transparent skin and paper-like mouth. They rarely weigh more than 1,5 kg and their gentle bite and bait-stealing habits tend to make them a nuisance.

'Yellows by float'
By Bill Steele

Dawn was breaking as we unloaded the boat from the car roof. The red bishop weavers were twittering in the nearby reed-bed. flashes of red among the green, while their dowdy hens whirred off across the river on unknown missions. Hadedahs, beaks curved, flapped down river as a lone brown 'Hamerkop' stood still as a statue and occasionally speared at small fry in the shallows. Tumbling masses of green willow caressed the river, ornamented here and there with white candy tufts of egret. The plop of rising yellow-fish pushed oily whirls across the glassy river.

We were at the Vaal River below the barrage. We were after large-mouth yellow-fish and hopeful that we would find some of the large specimens further downstream. Finding them is half the battle and to aid us with our search we had come equipped with a fish-finding echo-sounder. We were going to fish with float tackle and crushed crab and paste bait.

John was busy fitting up the echo-sounder as I tackled up. We had brought 4-m imported hollow glass-fibre rods. We fitted up

Mitchell fixed-spool reels loaded to the lip with 3 kg Platil Strong line and slipped on porcupine quill floats big enough to take five BB split shot. Finally we clinch-knotted size 8 'Model Perfect' hooks direct to the end of the line. Float fishing is possibly the most sensitive method of detecting a bite, as the commonly used ledgering methods do in fact fail to register many of the small movements which the yellow-fish can make. Once tackled up, we loaded the boat with our rods, keep net, landing net, bait and anchors and rowed off downstream.

We were looking for a spot which experience told us would hold yellow-fish. Typically, this is a gravel or rocky bottom with a fair current flowing over it. The shape of the bottom is important too. What we wanted was about 3 m of water over a bottom which shelved quite fast and ended in a ridge rising rapidly to shallow water. Food particles settle in a situation like this: they are caught up just before the ridge starts. Yellow-fish are well aware of this and usually such spots hold a fair head of large feeding fish. Our echo-sounder has an alarm and we had set this to operate at 3m. In consequence we could ignore it completely unless the alarm stopped. If that happened we would be over deep water which we could search thoroughly. Reading the echo-sounder requires a little practice since it shows differing patterns for the various types of river-bed. A rocky bottom shows up as a hard line whereas mud gives a broad pattern.

To search the whole river would have taken weeks, but we searched only the bends in the river. The current coming up against the bank cuts deep into the river-bed on the bends, washes away the mud and scours out the gravelly spots we were seeking.

After searching for an hour we finally found the type of river-bed contour we were looking for. The echo-sounder showed thin lines as fish moved in and out of the ultrasonic beam. It looked very much as though we had a perfect set-up for yellow-fish.

Keeping as quiet as possible, we drifted over our chosen spot and once well past it we rowed back in a broad circle and anchored 20 m above it. Yellow-fish are quite skittish and we did not wish to scare them. We anchored broadside to the stream, using both anchors for stability.

John baited up with crab and I put on paste about the size and shape of a 50-cent piece. The paste was a well-tried recipe of bread, crushed onion and cochineal to turn it red. We set the floats to put the bait about 10 cm over the river-bed. We were 'trotting' the floats, that is allowing them to go down river with the current. At the end of the swim-down we held the lines and allowed the bait to hover temptingly in the current for a few minutes.

After half an hour of fishing in this way we got some action. My float stopped, leant over and slid across the surface and stopped again. After a few seconds it moved again and silently disappeared. I struck, the rod arched and the reel clutch screamed like a scalded cat as the fish headed for some rocks 30 m away. It was moving fast and as I applied side-strain it stopped and turned in a flurry of spray and moved off to my right. The rod bucked and the line sang in the slight breeze as the big yellow reacted to the alien pull on its mouth. He made a long run, forcing the clutch to scream in protest. He was headed for clear water and I let him run another 30 m before again turning him.

Yellow-fish really fight hard, harder than a trout, but they fight with wild runs and great bursts of power. The fish turned and headed straight for me, but the high-speed Mitchell kept me in contact and the hook held. He came past the boat and headed for some sunken willows on our left. Again he was turned and forced into the open water. The fight was getting slower; he was slogging it out on the bottom as the rod bucked and throbbed in my hand. Eventually he came up wallowing like a golden pig, his shining armour scales glinting in the early morning sun. It was a fish of 5¼ kg in fine condition. I slipped him into the keep net and carried on fishing.

John's float slid silently under and he struck . . . no yellow-fish this time. The fish was heading smoothly out into the river at a steady speed. The reel clutch was singing as John tried side-strain and clamped down with finger pressure on the Mitchell spool rim. No reaction from the fish: it kept on, not deviating one inch from its chosen course. 'It must be a barbel, and a big one!' said John. 'Just look at the power . . . I cannot budge it'. The fish was well down and by now half of John's 200 m of line had gone but still the fish swam on! 'Do you want to lift the anchors and follow it?' I volunteered. 'No we will frighten the yellows, and I am after yellows today', he replied. 'Anyway, perhaps it will turn soon'.

John increased the pressure to maximum. His rod started pulsing as the fish put on power. Like a pistol shot the line parted it was over! The mystery fish had gone. 'I'll come back for that one with a rotten chicken and my sea tackle . . . must have been enormous', he said.

These big barbel can sometimes be a menace on light tackle, but we had been lucky. It had moved quickly out of our swim with minimum disturbance to the feeding yellows.

John changed to paste, hoping to avoid further barbel and we carried on fishing.

We had caught five more yellow-fish, all about 2 kg, when John's float stood up and lay flat. He hit it with a wrist-flick strike. The bait had to be in the fish's mouth for the float to lay over. The hook went home! This was something different: it made short runs and John's rod tip was jagging up and down furiously. There was none of the dashing fight one expects from a yellow-fish. It was soon played out and netted. 'It's a mud-fish, and a nice one too'; John said. So it was, it weighed 1,4 kg. It was sharp-nosed and silver deep in body and fat. It was an unusual catch. We normally expected to find mud-fish in almost still water.

It was a red-letter day: the yellow-fish came steadily to the net throughout. What more could an angler ask for? An idyllic setting, quiet, utterly private, and surrounded by wildlife and fabulous fishing. Such days are rare treasures to store away and recall to mind in quiet moments.

As dusk approached we changed from red to yellow floats for better visibility. The fishing had slowed and we thought that the huge barbel had returned. As we discussed the possible effects of large predatory fish like the barbel, John's float vanished and he struck. The line tore off his reel as the fish made a determined dash out into the river. It made several long powerful runs, further than a yellow would run, but distinctly slower. It was obviously large, it was difficult to turn and the runs were very long. It was rapidly becoming dark and I dug the torch from my tackle bag in anticipation of netting the fish. I had another 20 minutes to wait before the fish broke surface in front of the boat. It smashed a huge tail on to the water and smothered us in spray. The water boiled as it went down for another run. Eventually it slid into the big net shining brassy in the torch beam.

Its body was knee-deep and fat, blue-black and bronze. It was a fine specimen of carp which weighed in at 12,7 kg. What a climax to a perfect day! John was still shaking from the exertion and firmly declared that he could not row the boat back. Anyway, I had had all the entertainment while he had been involved in a strenuous battle!

Having returned the fish to the water, we grabbed an oar each and rowed our way back to the car 4 km upstream. It had been a very good day and, with the water gliding by and only the occasional 'plop' of a rising fish to punctuate the steady creak of the oars, we relived the fights and the excitement.

Days like that are rare, but because they are rare we treasure them. We remember them on the blank days, we remember them in quiet moments and we wait knowing that soon there will be another day maybe even better.

5 Kurper

(better known as bream in Rhodesia)

There are four types. The blue or red-finned or large-mouth (Mossambica) is the most common and best known and grows to some 2½ kg in weight, with the average fish in the vicinity of 1¼ kg. The others are the Red-breasted *(Melanopleura)*, Vlei *(Sparmanii)* and the Canary kurper *(Serranochromis thunbergi)*.

Canary kurper

It seldom grows larger than 18 cm in length and, as far as the angler is concerned, is a pest which eagerly takes the bait and wastes valuable time. Its breeding habits are similar to those of the *Mossambica*.

Vlei kurper

This is another of the smaller species that seldom manage to grow to more than 15 cm in length. Its breeding habits are similar to those of the *Melanopleura*.

Feeding habits

As kurper eat algae and insects, you should choose a fishing spot on stony ground and near reeds rather than on muddy ground. Kurper feed during summer when they come into the shallow water. Kurper normally detest silted water. Thus, after heavy rains clearer spots should be sought. Kurper usually go off the bite once the sun goes down. Towards the end of summer, kurper start feeding excessively on algae to store up fat for the winter when they hibernate. The fish, which usually makes excellent eating, is then not worth retaining as the flesh becomes tainted with the flavour of rotting vegetation. The blue kurper is a greedy fish. The small blue will usually take the bait very quickly, whereas the big blue usually jerks the line once and then slowly sucks the bait. I have seen shoals of large kurper, particularly in autumn just before they hibernate, beat fry into a small area in the shallows where they attacked them. Under these conditions they will readily take a fly, particularly a Polystickle or Muddler Minnow which resemble the fry.

Breeding habits

Kurper usually spawn during October and November. Generally speaking, fish will not readily take a bait whilst they are spawning, and these months are therefor usually poor for kurper fishing. The female fish lays a few hundred eggs in a hollow which the male has made in the mud. The male then releases sperm over the eggs and fertilises them. The female large-mouth or blue kurper then gathers the eggs into her mouth where they hatch after three days. For the next day or two the baby kurper live off the yolk of the egg and for the next two or three weeks they stay close to the mother and swim in and out of her mouth in search of vegetation. They promptly take refuge in the parental mouth at the slightest sign of trouble. After this period they leave their 'home'.

The red-breasted kurper is not a mouth-breeder but lays

adhesive eggs in a hollow against the bank. The two parent fish are hard put to protect the eggs against other fish and forms of water life until they are hatched.

Size hooks

Use a no. 2 long-shank hook with barbs on the shank to hold the worm in place. Use a light sinker so that you can detect the bite more easily, and only one hook per rod, as the big blue is a powerful fighter which soon hooks up a trailing hook.

Length of trace

The trace should be 7,5 to 10 cm long and fixed about 15 to 30 cm above the sinker. Too long a trace will rest on the bottom and make it more difficult to detect a bite.

Bait

Kurper are usually caught on earthworms, but the big blue may also take a paste bait. When using worms, leave a wriggly tail hanging down from the hook: the movement attracts fish. Flying ants come out after the rains and two or three of these on the hook are irresistible to kurper. Once the kurper start feeding on flying ants they will take any bait that hits the water. Kurper can also be caught on a small spinner but this is not usually very successful. Kurper also feed on and will take other insect baits. An artificial fluorescent worm has recently been placed on the market but is not as effective as a natural bait. Anglers using a trout rod and fly, however, have had excellent catches.

Float-fishing

Kurper will often be seen moving close to the surface. Then try to use a small float with a short lead of between 30 and 90 cm. No sinker should be attached so that the float will respond to the

A Large-mouthed Kurper of about 1 kg – Tilapia mossambica

slightest nibble on the bait. The float can be made self-cocking by winding fine lead or copper wire around the lower stem. Kurper will often swim with the bait, so you should strike immediately the fish starts to swim away with the float or as soon as it pulls the float under the water. This applies equally when you are fishing with a running float with a sinker attached to the line. In order to ascertain the correct distance at which the float should be fixed, when you use this method, thread the line through one hole of a button and then pass the line through the eyes of the float so that the float slides freely on the line. Tie the sinker and hook to the line below the float. Loop the line about 1,2 m above the sinker and pass one end of the line across the middle of the loop. Thereafter weave a small piece of stick through the two halves of the loop and pull the loop tight around the stick. Do not make a knot in the line. The float will rest at the depth of your cast. You can adjust the depth of your bait by varying the distance at which you loop the stick. A piece of match-stick is particularly suitable. You can also adjust the depth by compressing the lower eye of the float with pliers and fixing a small swivel or even a whipping of nylon to the line. If the float lies perpendicularly, you know the sinker is not resting on the bottom. Bring in your line and adjust the distance of the stick from the sinker until the float lies flat on the water. When this happens, your sinker will be on the bottom. By making gradual adjustments you can ensure that there is no slack line leading to the float. The trace should be attached in the same way as it would be when you use a fixed sinker for carp, but when you use a float you should rather use split shot. The float will rise immediately you have a bite. The 'lift method', described in the section on float-fishing, is also very effective.

Striking

As kurper seldom run with the bait, the fish must be struck as soon as you feel it nibbling. You will feel a sudden pull on your line as the kurper takes the bait, but when the fish feels the resistance of the sinker it will release the bait. Lift your finger under the line (which must be kept fairly taut) and you will feel a slight movement on the line as the fish returns to eat the bait again. This is the time to strike the fish. You will soon be able to distinguish the gentle pull of a large blue kurper from the jerky tug of a canary kurper. If you find your bait is being eaten without any bite being detected or that you are striking unsuccessfully, shorten your trace until it is some 50 mm long. In this way, you will not only detect a bite much more easily, but the fish will also be able to find your bait more easily. If your trace is long the bait may be lying in some water vegetation.

Preparation of kurper

Kurper are excellent table fish. They are bony, however, and easier to eat when filleted. To fillet a kurper, slip the point of a knife along the whole of the back fin and along the centre bone and 'peel' the fillet away from the bone by holding the cut section away from the bone and cutting the remaining flesh with circular movements of the knife along the bone in the direction in which the rib bones are pointing. The fillets should be rolled in flour and salt and gently fried in butter. Fillets which cannot be used immediately should be salted and kept in the refrigerator.

6 Trout

Four types of trout are found in South African waters. They are brown trout *(Trutta)*, rainbow trout *(Gairdneri)*, tiger trout (a hybrid trout produced by brook trout males fertilising brown trout eggs) and golden trout (also to be found in some Natal waters).

Many books have been written on trout fishing and the object of this chapter is merely to give the beginner a general idea of how to go about trout fishing. Trout fishing is a special art in itself, unlike bottom-fishing where the angler can never be sure what type of fish will take his bait. The experienced trout fisherman will use his knowledge of the habits of the fish and the water conditions to obtain the best results, and it is a tribute to his skill that he is able to present the fly in such a manner that a trout will be tempted to take a tasteless bundle of tinsel and feathers.

A wet fly is one that is so tied that it sinks, whilst a dry fly is designed to float on the surface of the water. It is easier to fish the wet fly. The dry fly is more effective in rivers than in dams, although few South African rivers produce hatches of fly like the European rivers. In dams it is usually only effective during the evening rise. Brown trout are caught more readily on a dry than on a wet fly, however. Most anglers using a dry fly lose the fish by striking too soon. When the fish rises for the fly, don't strike immediately — wait for your leader to move and straighten. For some inexplicable reason a trout cannot reject a dry fly as quickly as it can a wet fly. When selecting a dry fly, remember that a rise may be caused not only by a hatch of fly from the water, but also by a land hatch which has been blown on to the water.

Rainbow and brown trout were brought from England and America and introduced into the rivers of the Cape in the 1890s. They did well, and most waters in South Africa, of which the temperature remains sufficiently cold, are now stocked with rainbow trout. In fact, the South African strain of trout eggs is now being exported to Europe and America on a large scale.

The habits of brown trout differ from those of rainbow trout. Brown trout grow larger, particularly in dams, and fight in a different way, tending not to jump but to bore down to the depths.

The larger brown trout tend to split into two feeding types. The first type feeds almost exclusively on the bottom — on snails, crustaceans and large insects. They become silver in colour and are very powerful fighters. Special techniques have been developed to catch them. They are normally only caught in 7 to 10 metres of water with a large nymph or snail imitation, right on the bottom. In fact they will even take an artificial fly that has been lying still on the bottom and run with it. The best fly to use for this type is an imitation dragon-fly nymph.

Trout of the other type tend to establish their own territorial area where they remain. As they grow larger they become carnivorous and will eat minnows and larger forms of water life, including moths and mice. Unlike rainbow trout, brown trout will at times feed all night. In the evening, a fly imitating a moth is very successful.

Very few rivers and dams in South Africa are stocked with brown trout.

Selecting tackle

Choose your tackle with great care so that the rod, reel and line balance. Inexpensive rods, reels and lines usually do not balance. If possible, be guided by an old hand.

Reel

The reel without line should balance the rod at a point 2,5 cm above the cork grip. The reel is the least important item of your trout tackle. As its function is largely limited to storing the line, there is no need to buy an expensive trout reel.

Rod

For river-fishing choose a rod 2,5 to 2,75 m in length made of either split cane or glass fibre. The cane rods are heavier but have a beautiful action. They must be carefully dried and hung after use, or they will soon warp. For dam-fishing the rod should be a foot or so longer. The rod should be flexible but not too whippy — that is, it should have a fast action with a reserve of power in the butt. The action of the tip is very important. Make a downward stroke and watch whether the tip quickly comes to rest or vibrates for a few seconds. In the latter case the rod does not have the required hooking power and many a trout that has risen for a fly will not be hooked or will be hooked so lightly that it will soon kick off.

An easy way to test the rod is to hold it vertical and move it sharply from side to side. If the rod forms a parabolic shape it will be an ideal all-rounder. If most of the bend is at the butt, the rod will be highly suitable for nymph-fishing. If most of the bend is at the tip smoothly running into the butt, the rod will be suitable for long-distance casting and general wet-fly fishing in still water.

The weight of the rod is important. Choose a light rod with fittings of the best quality. The modern carbon-fibre rods are the very best in this respect and are also superior in distance casting, striking ability and bite detection. There are also a number of makes of superb glass-fibre rods available in the R50 to R90 price range.

In time, you will need the various types of lines — a floating line for dry-fly fishing and fishing wet flies (such as buzzers) just below the surface of the water, a slow sinking line for shallow and still water conditions, and a fast sinking line for deep water or a fast flowing river.

There are various types of line, each with its own special use.

A weight-forward line has the weight concentrated in the front end. It is very suitable for long-distance casting and double hauling.

A double-taper line has a taper at both ends and is useful for dry-fly anglers who can turn the line around when the one end is worn. It can also be used to provide two shooting heads.

A sinking-tip line is so called because the first 3 metres sinks while the remainder floats. You can control the depth of your fly and rate of retrieve more easily with this line than with a slow sinking line. The strike is also easier. It is particularly useful on a windy day as it will not drift as rapidly as a floating line. A sinking line retrieved slowly will always end up catching water growth on the bottom, but a sinking-tip line will not.

A line with a floating tip and sinking back is little used. Its purpose is to drag a nymph along the bottom.

High-density fast-sinking lines have the big advantage in that one can cast into the wind as the area of line cutting through the wind is fairly low. A slow sinking line which is thicker and has more resistance, is not as effective when cast into the wind.

A lead-core line sinks very rapidly and is useful when fishing in very deep water. A level line has no taper and is relatively useless.

Any leader and tippet can be made to sink quickly by rubbing a mixture of Fuller's Earth and washing-up liquid on to it. You should knead such a mixture to the consistency of putty and carry a ball of it in your kit.

Line

I recommend that the beginner choose a weight-forward line (*i.e.* a line that is tapered forward) which sinks fast. It is essential that the weight of the line, that is the AFTM size, match that of the AFTM number on the butt of the rod which you propose to use with that particular line. If the number of the line does not match that of the rod, it will obviously be less effective and you will struggle to cast properly. The line should preferably be on the heavy side and about 22 to 27 m long. A minimum of 45 m of backing should be attached to your line, preferably a braided dacron line, which is inexpensive, or plain nylon line of 5 - 6 kg breaking strain. A tapered cast is then attached to your line which permits you to cast and drop the fly without causing a splash which will frighten away the trout.

The length of the tapered cast (which is made from nylon line) depends on whether you are fishing wet or dry, and on your method. When the water is calm and the water temperature high, you will have better results with a long cast up to 6 m. Generally, however, when I fish with a wet fly I keep the tapered cast slightly shorter than the length of the rod, as it is easier to handle. You can buy a ready-made tapered cast, or you can make up your own cast by tying together with the blood or double fisherman's knot, various strengths of line, as follows:

Approximately 30 cm of 10 kg breaking strain line coupled to about 30 cm of 6 to 7-kg breaking strain coupled to about 30 cm of 4 kg breaking strain coupled to about 30 cm of 2 to 3 kg breaking strain which makes up the rest of your cast. The fly is attached to the end of this line. It is better to buy a ready-made knotless tapered cast, however, as it does not become entangled as easily.

A dropper is made by simply leaving a large length of line after you have tied one of your knots to make up your cast. Tie your dropper fly on to this, approximately 1 m from the chaser fly.

A rod complete with reel and line should balance about 10 cm from the edge of the angler's hand as he grips the rod.

Feeding habits

Trout will eat insects and, where the supply of fly food tends to be inadequate, frogs, baby birds, fry, crabs, worms, beetles and even mice that have fallen into the water. In fact, trout will eat any living thing small enough for them to swallow.

Most mountain streams are fast running and shallow for the most part and therefore lack abundant weed growth which is the source of food for trout. Therefore, the trout rarely grow large. There is nevertheless great satisfaction in catching a trout and many an angler who has tried trout fishing will forsake other types of fishing for it.

In certain dams lacking sufficient water life, the larger trout have become bottom feeders and show little interest in flies, but they can be caught if the right fly is properly presented to them.

Breeding habits

Trout breed in most South African rivers if the climatic and natural conditions are suitable, but very rarely in a dam, unless it is fed by a stream running with a suitable clean gravel bottom. The eggs will not hatch if silt is allowed to settle on them: the parent fish will keep them clean by fanning movements of its tail until they hatch. Most South African trout are bred in hatcheries whence the rivers and dams are stocked.

Likely spots

It takes years of experience and careful observation to discover in which sections of a river or part of a pool a trout is likely to be found. Trout do not lie anywhere and everywhere in a river. They choose spots which not only afford a safe refuge if danger threatens, but also provide them with a reasonable amount of food. Trout prefer gently flowing water where they can hold their position against the current with the minimum of effort and where food is carried down by the stream at a gentle pace. Trout will alter their position in the river according to the season, the weather conditions and the depth of the water. You will normally find several trout in one pool. The choicest position, generally at the head of the pool, will be occupied by the largest trout. The middle-sized trout will lie near the middle of the pool, and the smallest trout are usually found at the end of the pool where the food supply is poor. If a trout is taken, its place will soon be taken by a trout from the 'lower rung of the ladder' which in its turn will remain there so long as food and shelter are available.

You will thus have to try each pool or likely stretch of water in a river, unless you spot a cruising trout or see the ring of a rising fish. One can hardly expect trout to be accommodating, but they are easier to approach if they are cruising in still deep water or in a slack current of a backwater.

The following are some of the spots where trout are likely to be found; in quiet water behind boulders either hidden or projecting out of the water; at the rough edges of a stream that has been divided by a boulder; at the edge of, rather than in the stream; at the end of a pool where the water pours down into the pool below; in a back eddy between the main current and the bank; along the lip of a deep pool; under bushes and invariably under an overhanging branch which dips into the water. In the last mentioned case, poke your rod through the loose branches and drop the fly into the water.

Fish upstream whenever you can, although it is easier to

retrieve your fly when fishing downstream, as trout generally lie with their heads upstream and are less likely to see the angler if he is going upstream. Furthermore, they are less likely to disturb the unfished water as a trout generally rushes downstream when hooked. After you have cast upstream, allow the fly to float down over the fish and only remove it once it has passed below your position.

In summer, trout in a dam tend to rise during three periods of the day – early morning, midday and late evening. In early morning and late evening the trout will move into the shallower water when your fly can be retrieved close to the surface. I have caught many large trout only a metre or two away from the bank at these times. Therefore I believe that at these times of the day it is not necessary to disturb the water by wading in. During the day you should concentrate on fishing your fly deep in deeper water. A weed-bed is always a likely spot: trout are constantly cruising along the edges of the bed in search of food. I have found a tadpole fly fished on a slow sinking line just above a weed-bed to be deadly during the day. The problem is to land the larger trout which dive into the weeds as soon as they are hooked. If the fish does become firmly lodged in the weed, one of the few ways to move it is to give it slack line until it swims out again.

Four types of flies are used for trout – Dry flies, Wet flies, Nymphs and Lures.

☐ Dry flies are tied with the hackle at right angles to the hook so that they float on the surface of the water.

☐ Wet flies are tied with the hackle or wings pointing back to the bend of the hook so that they sink – they are fished beneath the surface of the water.

☐ Nymphs are tied to imitate the acquatic stage of development of various insects and are also fished beneath the surface of the water.

☐ Lures are fished like wet flies or nymphs. They are designed mostly to simulate small fish or larger subaquatic nymphs, e.g. dragon flies. Some are purely 'attractor patterns'.

A typical early September morning in the Machadodorp area, Eastern Transvaal

Flies

When choosing flies, never be tempted by gaudy colours as such flies usually only catch the fisherman who chooses them. There are of course exceptions to this rule, as in most things to do with fishing. The Mickey Finn is one such fly which is usually very successful when fished on a cold misty day.

Generally speaking, the plain dullish coloured flies give the best results. The following traditional pattern flies can usually be relied upon in any conditions: Walker's Killer, Mrs Simpson, Black Widow, Invicta and Invicta with red tail, March Brown, Connemara Black, Coch-y-Bondhu, Hardy's Favourite, Dusty Miller, Gold Ribbed Hare's Ear Nymph, Mallard and Claret and Parson's Glory.

Local anglers who tie their own flies have experimented with various new patterns, and devised some deadly flies. I can thoroughly recommend the Taddy, the Machadodorp, the Vlei Kurper and the Scampy (see the illustration plate on flies).

The materials for these flies are:

The Taddy

Hook: no. 10
Silk: black.

The body: black squirrel tail fibres.
The fibres are tied around the hook, pointing forward past the eye. They are then pulled back loosely over the shank so as to make the fibres bow and achieve the right head shape. They are tied in at the body so that the front portion comprises the tail of the fly. Three or four coats of venglaze or polyurethane should be applied to the head. This fly has no body tie.

Machadodorp

Hook: no. 6 to 10
Silk: black
Body: grey chenille
Hackle: iron blue cock feather
Wing: grey duck wing quill.

Vlei Kurper

Hook: no. 6 long shank
Body: yellow rayon floss with fluorescent red wool for the thorax (front quarter of the body)
Wing: dark green buck-tail tied on top of medium green buck-tail
Ribbing: silver wire
Throat hackle: yellow buck-tail. In addition, 2 small pieces of copper lurex are tied on the side
Head: black varnish with white eyes painted on either side.

The Scampy

Hook: no. 6
Silk: black
Body: red or yellow chenille.
Rib: 3 lengths of Peacock Herl.
Wing: yellow-pink buck-tail with an under-wing of fur from my toy

pom, Scampy. (Any long gingery fur will do as a substitute)

Tail: Yellow-pink buck-tail with fur of toy pom

Throat: Small bunch of fur of toy pom

Head: yellow varnish with gold dust dabbed on.

Mike's Secret

Hook: long shank size 6 to 8.

Silk: yellow

Body: yellow floss

Ribbing: flat gold wire

Tail: yellow marabou feather

Wing: orange squirrel tail tied on the top and sides of the hook

Throat Hackle: yellow marabou fluff

Head: the head should be painted with three coatings of polyurethane varnish.

The size of the fly you use depends on the type of water, and on the type and size of the insect or fish your fly resembles. When using a dropper, ensure that the chaser fly is usually bigger than the dropper fly. Use a smaller fly when fishing a stream.

It is a much debated question whether bigger trout tend to be caught on bigger flies. Certainly, smaller trout tend to be caught on smaller flies, but I have caught many large trout on very small flies, including the Southern Transvaal record, a fish of 3,58 kg on a no. 10 hare's ear nymph.

Trout have been shown to appreciate colour. They have been known to reject a fly of a particular colour but greedily take the same fly with a slight colour variation. It does not follow that a bright fly should be used on a dull day, and vice versa.

There is one general rule in choosing a particular type, colour or size of fly. Try to use flies that simulate the insects or insect larvae forms present at the time and on which the trout are likely to be feeding. Certain types of flies are painstakingly designed to resemble the appearance and action of a particular type of insect or larvae form. Alternatively, you may try using an attractor pattern fly that has been proven successful. The expert will know which fly to select. The newcomer to the sport will learn that instead of rushing to cast a fly into the water, it pays to spend a leisurely few minutes enjoying the beauty of the country-side and studying the water life before choosing the fly closest in appearance to the type of insect seen in the water.

The next problem is to know how to fish that fly so that it convincingly resembles that insect. You must know at what depth of water to fish the fly and at what speed the natural insect or larvae form moves, so that your rate of retrieval and the action of your fly simulate the natural food you are trying to imitate.

I don't believe that one can categorically state that a particular fly will be successful in given conditions. Fish, especially trout, are unpredictable, but you will reduce the element of chance by selecting a fly that resembles as closely as possible the particular type of water life.

Bill Steele has prepared the following 'hatch table' representative of insects found in the Dullstroom/Belfast area in the Eastern Transvaal. This was collected over two seasons and whilst it may be incomplete and the hatch times may vary, it is fairly representative and most useful. Any angler keeping a fishing diary could do the same and make a worth-while contribution to trout fishing. The sudden drops in temperature may reduce hatches to almost nothing, but the nymphs will always be there.

		Sept	Oct	Nov	Dec	Jan	Feb	March	April
- -	Sporadic light hatch								
X	Heavy hatch								
XX	Dense hatch								
Caenis		--	XX	X	X	XX	X	--	X
Sepia Dun									X
May-fly, Brown body, Green wing			X	--	X				
May-fly, Green body, Pale yellow wing							X	--	
May-fly, Pale green body, Very pale yellow wing		X							
Tiny sedge (Size 16)		X	--		X	--			
Orange sedge						--	X	--	
Large sedge (Size 10)		X	--					--	X
Small silver-horn		X	X	--		X	--		
Black reed smut				--	X	--			
Brown corixid		--	X	X	XX	XX	X	--	
Tiny olive corixid									X
Small black buzzer		X						--	X
Large black buzzer					--	X	X	--	
Claret buzzer			X	--				X	X
Large olive buzzer				--	X	XX	X	--	
Deep olive buzzer		--				X	X		
Damsel fly				--	X	X	X	--	
Dragon-flies			--	X	X	X	X	X	--
Small rana tadpole					X	X	X	X	
Black ant			X	X					
Vlei kurper fry					X				

Flies may be categorised into two classes: those resembling natural foods, which are tied so as to resemble them, and lures which do not resemble any natural form of food. There are several theories as to why a trout will take a lure. It does so probably because it was hungry or curious or had been made aggressive. It may be a reflex defensive action or a combination of these factors.

I have found that a lure should be retrieved by a series of pulls and pauses rather than at a steady and constant pace. Make sure that the fingers of your other hand have lightly but securely caught the line you are retrieving, or you will not be able to strike when a fish bites, when you have stopped the retrieval for a moment. Not only will you lose the fish, but you will find your fingers have been cut. Plastic insulation tape wound over the crook in your fingers helps protect them.

As not every lure will catch fish, it follows that there are certain features in a particular lure that are attractive to fish.

It will be worth your while carrying out an autopsy on the first trout you catch and inspecting the contents of its stomach to see what it has been feeding on. Put the contents into a clean bowl of water and learn to identify snails, the main types of nymphs, blood-worms (the larval form of the midge), chironomid pupa (more commonly known as buzzers or midge pupa), caenis and the like.

In time you will understand what a trout is doing when it rises, leaps out of the water, swirls or otherwise disturbs the water. You will learn to tell when trout are feeding on hatching pupae just below the surface so that the water suddenly boils with the movement of rising fish. If you now present a fly resembling the pupa and imitate the action of the hatching pupa, you should have your bag limit in record time.

Dropper fly

The experienced angler may on occasion try to fish with two flies attached to his cast. The additional fly or flies are attached to the cast by a short dropper. (Refer to the chapter on knots.) The blood-knot or four-turn water-knot is suitable for a dropper. One end of line is about 12 cm long, to which the other fly is attached, while the other line end is cut off. The flies should vary in size, the largest usually being attached to the end of the line so that it gives the impression that the larger fly is chasing the others. This excites the fish. The use of an extra fly also helps to discover which fly the fish prefer on that particular day.

I have found that a large dark coloured fly chasing an orange coloured dropper fly is an excellent combination in lures. My favourite combination is a Walker's Killer or Mrs Simpson coupled with a Fuzzy Wuzzy (preferably tied with a blue-throat hackle).

If the water is discoloured the fish will not be able to see the fly easily and results will be poor. A yellow or orange fly should, therefore, be used under these conditions.

Casting

Casting properly is an art that requires considerable practice. The better your casting technique, the better will be your presentation of the fly to the fish, and the more likely you are to catch it. To present your fly correctly, you must be able to drop your fly accurately and gently at the required position, and cast it at the greatest possible distance so as to be able to retrieve it, simulating the desired action or movement.

In fly-casting the line is so weighted that you actually cast the line while the fly is carried along with it. The weights to be cast are distributed throughout the length of the line.

Sufficient force must be applied to the rod to give the line the momentum to carry it out. The following stages must be observed:-

Set up your tackle and find an open area, such as your lawn. Pull out about 8 m of line, pick up your rod and stand with your feet at an angle of 45° to the point you wish to cast to.

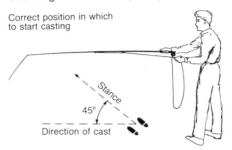

Correct position in which to start casting

Stance

45°

Direction of cast

The back cast

The line must be straight out behind the rod tip in the direction in which you wish to cast.

The back cast is made with the right elbow and shoulder, if you are right-handed. Lift the rod up and back, picking up speed as you take it back. The line is held and controlled in your other hand, and as the rod approaches a vertical position (12 o'clock), pull the line you are holding in the other hand downwards as far as you can comfortably pull it. The line will be coming towards you in the air. Use your shoulder to bring the rod back and pivot your elbow until the rod is vertical. Stop it in this position.

The movement is brisk and continuous and the rod must be made to bend with the weight of the line as you take it back. You can now tip the rod back to one o'clock by bending your wrist so that the rod is in position to retrieve the force of the forward cast. Practice this movement until the line shoots behind you parallel to the ground and in line with the rod tip. You must now pause for a second or two while the line is brought back, and straighten out before starting the forward cast.

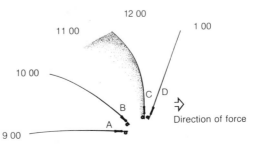

The back cast

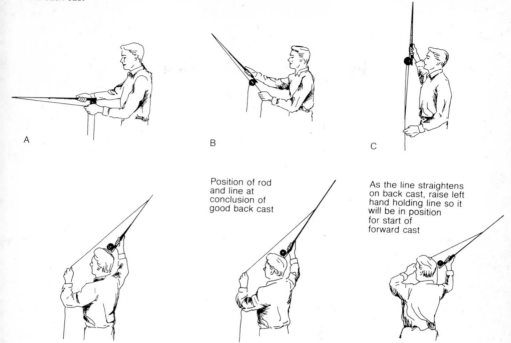

A

B

C

Position of rod
and line at
conclusion of
good back cast

As the line straightens
on back cast, raise left
hand holding line so it
will be in position
for start of
forward cast

D

The forward cast

Your right hand should now be slightly higher than your shoulder and your left hand, holding the line close to you body.

Quickly bring your whole shoulder and elbow forward until the rod is in the eleven o'clock position and then stop, simultaneously lowering your left hand with the line still held in it. Learning to stop dead at the end of the back and forward cast is the secret to good fly-casting as this gives the rod tip the momentum to increase the speed at which the line moves.

Practise the forward movement until the line straightens in front of you. Then lower your arm and rod and allow it to fall on to the ground. If the line does not straighten, you are probably waving it around instead of making it do the essential work. If, after a few casts you find that your leader has a few knots in it, you know that you are dropping the tip of the rod and pushing it.

Practise these movements until you have achieved the right action, and you know the exact timing of the pauses in the back and front stop positions.

You are now ready to false-cast and work out line to cast further.

False casting is so called because the fly does not touch the water on the forward cast. Make the required back and forward cast and as the line straightens out on the forward cast, start the back cast. You must not allow the line to slip through the rod rings until you are ready to shoot the line out with your final cast. Do not try to cast more than 10 m until you are quite proficient. This distance is adequate to catch most of your trout.

If you hit the water or ground with your back cast, you are taking your rod too far back. Remember, it must not move further back than one o'clock and further forward than eleven o'clock.

You can now work out line by releasing a metre of line at a time while making the back cast, until you have 10 m of line out which you release on your next forward cast.

Timing and muscle control are the secret of good casting, and in time you will be able to drop your fly into a saucer 10 m away.

The forward cast

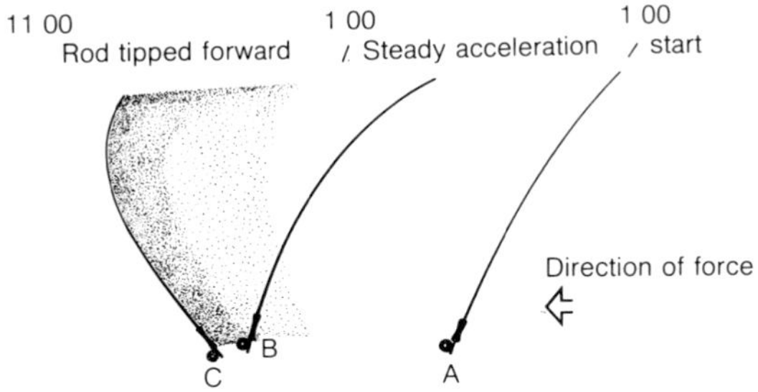

11 00

Rod tipped forward

1 00
/ Steady acceleration

1 00
/ start

Direction of force

B
C
A

C

B

A

Double-hauling and the shooting-head
By Bill Steele

In response to the many enquiries I have received whilst fly-fishing at various dams in the Eastern Transvaal, I have finally put pen to paper and will attempt to explain the fundamentals of long-distance fly casting.

The technique I am describing here is the 'double-haul', particularly with reference to 'shooting-head' application.

The first explanation is due, I think, to the commonly posed question 'Why is it necessary to cast 40 m or more?' In answer, I would say that increasing your distance by any amount is surely going to increase your flexibility and your ability to cover more fish. Additionally, it is most important to spend as much time fishing the water as possible. As your distance increases you will spend more time fishing, less time casting and will additionally cover more fish. On this basis, it is not unreasonable to expect higher returns for your efforts. If your maximum cast is presently 18 to 20 m, your chances of attracting a trout stationed 40 m out are practically nil – the trout might just as well be a kilometre away.

The old maxim of 'fine and far off' is also pertinent: at 40 m the trout has far less chance of detecting your presence. In these days, when angling pressure is increasing considerably, wading fly-casters undoubtedly force the fish to move away from the shore.

The man with the long-distance cast can expect a considerable advantage over his fellow anglers. The technique is not irrelevant to stream fishing either. Many are the occasions when a long cast will enable you to pick up a trout which would normally be unreachable. Many advantages will suggest themselves to the thinking man. One which I have found most productive is in connection with chironomid hatches (buzzers).

These flies normally hatch over water with a minimum depth of 2 m, usually on a gradually sloping bottom. To place a hatching pupa imitation over the trout almost invariably requires a 30 to 40 m cast. Since this is undoubtedly one of the most productive methods of fishing, the advantage of the long-distance cast is immediately obvious.

The first principle of long-distance casting is to acquire a correctly balanced outfit. Buying the very best equipment (not necessarily the most expensive) will also pay dividends. There are some beautiful compound taper rods available on the market today, many specifically designed for shooting-head casting. The floppy action rod should be avoided at all costs (the so-called wet-fly action). What you need is a stiffish fast dry-fly action rod, capable of picking up and aerializing a complete fly-line if necessary. There are few rods which will meet the requirements needed, but Abu, Hardy, Connolon, Bruce & Walker and Don's, to name but a few, all produce rods designed for the job. An important point to bear in mind is the actual rod weight. A suggested maximum of 170 gms – 125 gms is ideal.

The AFTM casting weight of the rod is ideally 9, but AFTM 7 or 8 is quite serviceable. This AFTM rating is most important: any rod which does not give its rating should be avoided. The AFTM number refers to the line weight which the rod is designed to cast. This weight refers to the first 10 m of line only (the shooting-head length) and this is the line size which you will purchase.

If your stockist keeps shooting-heads, you may as well purchase one outright to start with. Unfortunately, ready-cut shooting-heads are not normally available, and in this event you must purchase a full-length double-taper line and cut off your shooting-head. It is a good idea to share with an angling friend. In terms of usefulness, a floating line is the most adaptable and this should be your first purchase.

Once you have acquired your line, cut off 9 m from either end. Should you be unable to acquire the correct line size, you can go one size lower and cut off 10 m, but this is not recommended. To the tapered end of the line, splice approximately 60 cm of 9,98 kg line and to the other end splice on 100 m of the softest 9,98 kg nylon you can find. Platil Soft and Damyl Royale are both very good lines for this job. This splice should be made with a nail knot and then varnished over preferably with a polyurethane varnish.

Wind the line on to your reel, which should be light in weight and preferably just filled to within 3 mm of the spool rim. The modern multiplying fly-reels are ideal for this job. High-speed line recovery can be a boon to the long-distance caster.

A last word on lines – buy the best you can afford. The shooting-head is subjected to higher speeds and stresses than ordinary fly-lines. Only a good quality plastic coated line can withstand this hard wear. You can however expect 4 to 5 years life from a good line; a poor line will probably not see the season through.

Now you have your outfit and are ready to commence practise, but first tie on 2 m of leader and an old fly with the hook point snipped off. In this way you will avoid destroying or cracking the point of your shooting-head. Use a field or a large garden for practise and go there as often as possible until you feel that you have reached a point where you can cast well by reflex. Practise is very necessary in the early stages. Ideally you should practise at least one hour per day.

The basic back cast

Commence by working out all the shooting-head and pull off about 3 m of backing which should lie on the ground devoid of snags.

Lay out the shooting-head in front of you and hold the backing firmly in your non casting hand (your line hand). There should be about 1 m of backing between the head and the rod tip. Hold the rod in the 11 o'clock position. In a smooth accelerating movement move the rod from the extended arm position back to your shoulder, bending your elbow in order to ensure that the rod point moves parallel to the ground. As your arm draws opposite to your ear, commence to move your shoulder muscles to bring the rod back further still and finally flick the rod from 11 o'clock to 1 o'clock and then allow the rod to drift to the 2 o'clock position. Use the full amount of movement available to you – the arm should be extended at the commencement and at the end of the cast.

Fig. 1. The back cast
The line should travel out smoothly behind you. The purpose of the drift is to remove the waves from the line so commonly seen in dry-fly casting with its abrupt 1 o'clock stop. These waves

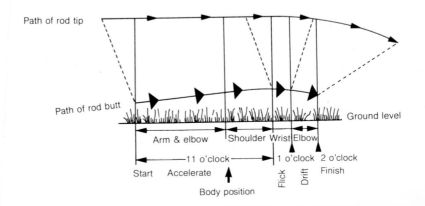

Fig. 1

74

can absorb as much as 50% of the energy produced in the ensuing forward cast – their elimination is therefore a must. Things to watch at this point are:

(a) Do not sweep with the rod: it must be upright throughout the movement.

(b) Do not allow your wrist to twist, as this sets up horizontal waves in the line.

(c) Do not use every ounce of energy your possess. Although a fast movement, it is essentially leisurely and relaxed.

(d) If you want to watch your back cast (it helps to do this), do not twist your body, which also causes horizontal waves. Instead, put your head back and look over your shoulder. Any turning of the head or body must be avoided.

The basic forward cast

This time you will complete the back as before, but the instant the line straightens out behind you, parallel with the ground at rod-tip height, you will commence the forward cast. Timing is very important and you must practise for commencement of the forward cast before the line starts to fall. The forward movement commences with an easy return of the rod to the 1 o'clock position as the line straightens out behind your. Once the line is straight the rod is punched forward, still in the 1 o'clock position, to the extent of arm and forward shoulder movement. Again this is a smooth accelerating movement culminating in a fast wrist flick to the 11 o'clock position at which point the rod is stopped dead.

Fig. 2. The forward cast.
The moment the rod stops, release the backing. The shooting-head should fly forward until stopped by the reel.

Things to watch:

(a) a, b and c as for the back cast. There is a tendency to overdo things by putting everything one has into the forward cast. This invariably ruins the cast as a result of rod backlash and irregular movement. Take it easy, relax and you should be able to reach 30 m after practise.

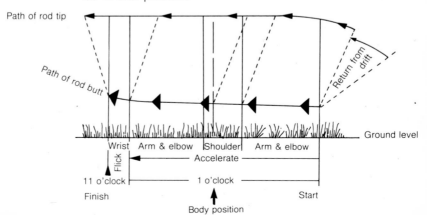

Fig. 2

75

(b) Don't pull off metres of backing yet! Practise the short cast with 3 m of backing.

(c) If your line comes off in a twisted heap it is almost surely due to moving forward of 2 o'clock before reaching the wrist-flick stage. This results in a double loop being thrown – a real knot-tier!

(d) Line arc: If everything is correct you should be throwing a tight loop which will cut through the air.

(e) When fishing, you must avoid unnecessary line splash; hence prior laying-out of the shooting-head is not feasible. You should therefore practise working the line out in the air. When you do this, make a point of following the rules of casting. All your casting actions should be smooth and controlled.

Fig. 3. Good loop shape and bad loop shape.
Well, after practice you will have discovered that you can make 30 m without the double-haul – probably an already noticeable improvement. Now we come to the 'haul' proper. Once mastered, this skill will last you all your life. Not only will you be able to cast tremendous distances with the wind behind you, but you will also be able to cast 25 m or so into the teeth of a gale. This will permit you to fish the most productive water on a windy day, *ie.* downwind, and probably to have the whole bank to yourself as an added bonus.

Fig. 3

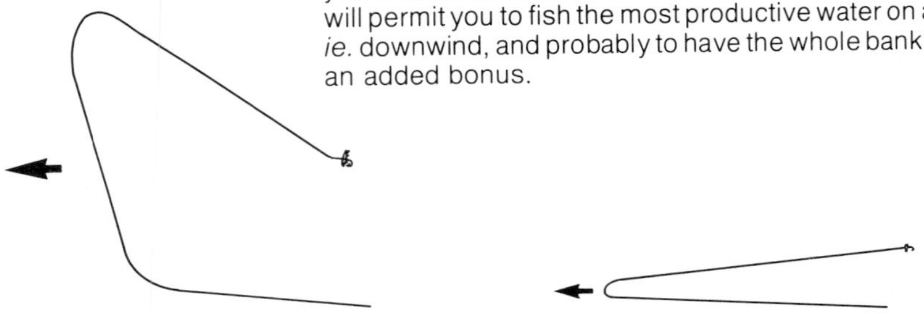

Bad loop shape

Good loop shape

The back haul

This is quite simple compared with the forward haul. In a way this is the most useful of the two hauls because it enables you to put a straight back cast into the wind. This is essential to all casting – your back cast must be good.

Commence your back cast as before, but this time move the hand holding the backing (your line hand) forward at the same time as you move the rod backward. In other words, simply spread your arms. The faster you move your 'line-hand', the greater will be the speed of the shooting-head. You will notice greater flexing of the rod and will feel the power building up as the back cast straightens. Finally, as the line straightens you will feel it tugging at your hand. At this point allow the line to pull your arm up to the rod. As you make the forward cast, move your line arm with the rod and release at 11 o'clock as before. Practise until you have mastered this. You should already notice that the line would go further if you let it. However, as before, practise with a short amount of backing.

Fig. 4

Fig. 4. The back haul

Things to watch for:

(a) In the back haul your line arm should be extended at the end of the haul. Any haul helps, but a long haul is most effective.

(b) Line control: it takes practise to handle the nylon backing. Do not be dismayed if it slips from your hand in the early stages.

(c) Try to keep your backing from rod tip to shooting-head down to one metre or less. Too much aerialized backing can lead to all sorts of difficulties.

(d) Put the speed in the correct place. Swishing or wooshing noises by the rod indicate too much speed by the rod arm. The hauling arm is the one which should move fast.

The forward haul

This is the movement which produces the great distance which is the mark of the shooting-head caster. In theory this is a very simple movement, but in practice it requires superb timing and control. It is the hardest of the four basic movements, but once mastered is the most rewarding.

The forward haul is applied during the time the forward wrist-flick from 2 o'clock to 11 o'clock is performed. Very few people manage it precisely: most of us commence the haul a split second too early. However, you should aim at hauling all the way from the rod (the finished hand position in the back haul) to as far back as you can move your line hand.

See Figs 5A and 5B

This whole movement shoud take place during the wrist-flick. The line is released at the end of the wrist-flick. You will hear the shooting-head whistle through the air; the backing will come up hard against the check, and it will be very obvious that the line is moving very fast.

Things to watch for:

(a) There is an even greater tendency to put everything one has into it. Don't, it will ruin the cast. High speed will give you greater distance, but it must be a relaxed high-speed movement. Tense muscles do not move smoothly.

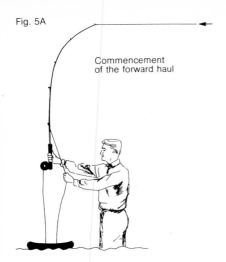

Fig. 5A

Commencement
of the forward haul

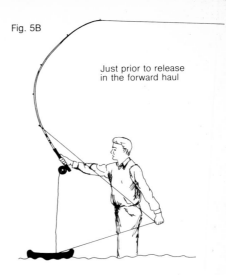

Fig. 5B

Just prior to release
in the forward haul

(b) Don't come forward on tiptoe in an attempt to get further. You
will simply cause the rod tip to drop and everything will land in a
heap.

General points

When practising, rest as soon as you feel tired. You must obey
this rule at all times. Tired muscles will spoil your style and
introduce bad habits.

On the water, use a line raft or even a bucket for your backing.
If you do not do this, you will find your backing constantly caught
up on the bottom and your cast will be shortened. A bicycle
inner tube inflated in a flat polythene sack is a simple yet effective
line raft.

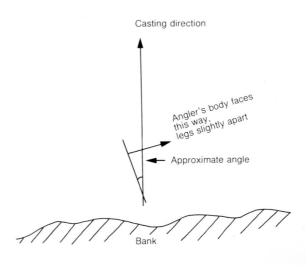

Casting direction

Angler's body faces
this way,
legs slightly apart

Approximate angle

Bank

Do stretch your backing before fishing: this definitely reduces backing tangles. If you can get it, use flattened monofil for backing.

Never lay your shooting-head on your backing – it will tangle!

Do pull off an additional 2 m of backing and lay it in the water – this allows for movement during casting.

Should you find everything going wrong, relax and cast leisurely. You will probably find your distance will increase. You do not need big muscles for long-distance casting; aim at a relaxed style which you can keep up all day long.

Try to get into the habit of positioning your body at an angle to your rod. When casting with the wind, aim high: the line loop should climb at an angle of approximately 5 degrees. When casting into a wind, aim downhill.

You must not expect to reach the magic 40 m first time out. This takes time and practise. However, once achieved it is very rewarding. There will be days when only those who have mastered the double-haul will catch trout. On days like that the reward is truly proportionate to what you put into it in the form of practise, practise, and more practise.

Retrieving the fly

The correct action in retrieving the fly is vital. As I have mentioned, the pace and manner of the retrieval (*i.e.* short pulls and pauses, a constant and steady retrieval or a nymphing action) and the depth at which the fly is fished, are some of the most important factors that will determine the size of your bag.

Some experts have made a careful study of water insects and know the exact speed and depth at which they move, and retrieve their fly accordingly. The excellent results they achieve speak for themselves.

I hold my rod at a slight angle almost parallel to the water as I retrieve. In this way I keep adequate contact with the fly but allow the rod to bend under the strain of a sudden hard take. If the rod is pointing straight to the fish, it may smash the leader on a hard take, as the inexperienced angler cannot instinctively control the line while letting it gently slip through his fingers. The main line must be caught gently with the fingers holding the rod, or else you will have no control on the line and be unable to strike when you have a take, particularly during a pull and pause retrieval. To begin with, you may allow the retrieved line to lie at your feet, but this tends to become entangled in every piece of grass or twig. As you become more proficient, you should be able to wind up the line into a shank in your other hand. A line tray tied to your waist is useful, particularly when wading. You can simply let your line fall into this.

If you wish the fly to sink deeper, or if there is a fastish current, you may weight the fly by fixing a piece or two of shot to the line. Do not make the mistake of placing the shot too near to the eye of the hook, however, as this will spoil its natural action.

When fishing a nymph on the bottom, the action of the retrieval should resemble the nymph rising a few centimetres off the bottom and falling again. You will simulate the desired action by repeatedly raising and dropping your rod a few centimetres at a time and retrieving the slack line.

The faster the rate of retrieval, the more violent the take. A trout will usually swim at a pace just fast enough to take a moving fly. There are, of course, exceptions. An angler is 'smashed up' mostly because the trout, having taken the fly in its mouth, is moving off in a different direction, whilst the angler is continuing to strip his line. The impact results in a 'smash' take. With the passing of the years you should develop the anticipation and sensitivity required to minimise being so 'smashed'.

The tip of a floating line (but never of a shooting-head) must be greased to prevent it sinking. You will not see many of your takes if the tip of your line has sunk and is out of sight: a trout can accept and reject a nymph without moving the leader or line. Usually, however, you will notice when the leader is being interfered with as the fly is pulled or lifted: you must strike at the faintest movement of the leader.

Trout which are well fed become lazy and prefer the food being brought to them to swimming out of their water level to obtain it. In a fast moving river the bigger fish will lie in the deeper sections. They are not likely to move unless the food actually comes to them or unless it looks particularly appetising.

One should fish with the fly close to the surface in the early morning and evening, as trout normally feed close to the surface at this time of day. If you find the trout are taking short (striking the fly but not taking it), try a jerk retrieval or change the size or pattern of the fly. If there are no takes, try another type of fly.

Immediately you feel a strike, briskly lift the tip of the rod or move it sideways to set the hook. At the same time, control the line gently in the crook of your fingers, as the trout suddenly dashes off when it feels it is hooked. Many anglers disagree with this view and feel that the easiest way to lose a trout is to strike it immediately you feel a take. Their advice is to let the fish run for a foot or two before striking, as this ensures the fish has the hook in its mouth. I have found, however, that I hook more trout by striking immediately, as a trout has a very sensitive mouth and will reject the fly immediately it feels resistance. Even if the line appears to be snagged, you should strike – by bringing your wrist back sharply – as trout also tend to hold the fly for a few seconds before discarding it. These bites usually feel as if you have hooked a small piece of weed.

In time you will be able to distinguish every resistance and knock when retrieving, and you will instinctively know when you have snagged a piece of weed or other inanimate object or have had a take.

You should retrieve your fly to the point where you are standing: the fish will often follow and grab it as you are about to lift it out of the water.

The rod is flexible and will bend a foot or two as the trout swims away with the fly. Fight the fish on the rod, using your spare hand to retrieve the slack line. Never play the fish off the reel, or you will lose it as you cannot wind in fast enough. The trout should be played by holding the rod in the 2 o'clock position (except when the fish jumps) as the bend in the rod tires the fish. If the fish is large and runs, let the line out of your hand, controlling it so that there is always tension on the line. If the trout jumps away from you while you play it, immediately drop the tip of the rod, otherwise the trout may break the cast by striking it with its tail, or the fly will be torn from its mouth if there is too much tension, even though the weight of the fish may only be a fraction of the breaking strain of the cast. Once the fish falls back into the water, lift the tip of your rod so that the slack line is taken in. If the fish jumps in your direction, raise the tip of the rod a little to draw the slack line out of the way of the descending fish. Try to hold the line taut as the fish jumps, giving a little slack again as it hits the water. Many anglers are afraid to play a fish, especially when it jumps. Remember that a badly hooked fish is probably a lost fish, and a well hooked fish can be lost by timidity. Do not attempt to net the trout until it offers an easy chance or is so tired that it lies quite still on its side. Never bring the net towards the fish but gently guide the fish over the net.

Sight and movement

A trout is particularly sensitive to vibrations caused by movement on the bank. To obtain the best results you will have to approach a particular pool or spot carefully, keeping low and making use of all available cover. Where the stream is clear and the bank offers no cover, you should fish in the kneeling position and keep the rod low. Try to wear dark clothing that blends in with the background.

Trout have excellent eyesight and will flee from the slightest movement that may spell danger. A trout has monocular vision, that is it can see an object clearly with one eye and at the same time focus the other eye on another object. For these reasons, you should avoid wading. When the sun is behind you, be careful your shadow does not fall on the water, and also that your rod has no shiny or metal fittings likely to produce vivid flashes as you swish it through the air when casting. A grey or blue rod is preferable as it is almost invisible through water.

The average angler stops fishing when it becomes dark. This is when the expert will take most fish, however. As dusk sets in, take note of the terrain around you so that you can estimate distances and cast to the sound of a rising trout nearby. You will have to remember the dangerous obstacle- filled areas and play the trout by instinct and feel, keeping it in clear water. I find fishing in those moments of darkness before the moon rises the most exciting and challenging, as well as the most productive.

Trout are able to see a fly when it is dark. In fact, they can even distinguish between slight variations in colour in the dark. Recent research has shown that trout are very susceptible to colour and can see over a broader spectrum of light than man. Different colours will reflect different degrees of light to create different silhouettes. For this reason, fluorescent materials are important in fly-tying. For some reason which I cannot explain, it is more difficult to catch rainbow trout on a moonlit night or on an evening when the moon rises early.

Preparing a trout

Few anglers know how to clean a trout. In order to retain its delicate flavour, the trout should not be washed but wiped clean with a damp cloth after it has been gutted, and then gently fried in butter. Another excellent method is to slit the cleaned trout 3 or 4 times on each side and insert butter into the slits and abdominal cavity. Grease a baking dish and pour cherry brandy or wine into the dish to a quarter the depth of the trout. Sprinkle mace over it and bake. Delicious!

Choosing flies for still water
By Bill Steele

Suppose somebody said: 'From now on you are only allowed six different wet flies'. For the long-time angler this would mean the immediate submission to the dust-bin of 75% of the contents of his fly-box. But the beginner would very much like to know what is left in that fly-box! That is really the situation the author is placed in when asked to list the most successful flies. Indeed, there are flies which consistently prove more successful than others. My choice would be as follows: Walker's Killer, Taddy, Gold-Ribbed Hare's Ear Nymph, Muddler Minnow, Mickey Finn, and Invicta.

If asked to choose three more, I would settle for Black Buzzer, Whisky Fly, and Polystickle.

Just to round it up to ten, I would add the Black Marabou with Jungle Cock. Armed with these ten you should be able to catch trout under almost any circumstances, but you must know how each fly is properly used. I propose to outline the correct method for each fly and the circumstances in which each should be used.

Walker's Killer

This is probably the fly with the best reputation in South Africa. It is principally a day-time (as opposed to dusk or dawn) fly, which is most effective during the summer months when the water is warm. When wet, this fly simulates effectively most of the brown/sepia dragon-fly nymphs which are extremely common and a wholesome addition to the trout's diet. You will frequently find these nymphs in the stomach contents of the fish. I believe that a trout of any size, big or small, finds it impossible to pass up the opportunity of a fat juicy dragon-fly nymph; hence the effectiveness of this fly. The only thing they seem to like more is a small black tadpole (see Taddy).

The dragon-fly nymph spends his time crawling around the bottom of the lake or stream. Occasionally, he makes a short sharp dash after some other small animal or in order to move location. This is when the trout spots him and this is the movement you must imitate. The Walker's Killer should be fished deep in short 10 cm pulls. You should be prepared for fierce takes since the fish is usually moving fast when he hits the fly. I would not recommend a leader of less than 3 kg breaking strain, especially if you are fishing in still water.

The Taddy

This is a recent discovery, as far as South African flies go. It was invented by the author as a tadpole imitation and has shown itself to be as effective if not more so than the Walker's Killer. Principally, it simulates the small Rana type tadpoles, but is also accepted by the fish as an imitation of a buzzer, or a fry or as a silhouette imitation of some sedge pupae. It is effective at any time of day, but very good at dusk. It fishes well on its own, but when combined with the Walker's Killer (Taddy on the dropper) it becomes a real fish slayer. Strangely enough, the fish will nearly always hit the Taddy rather than the Walker's Killer. A possible explanation derives from the hunting instinct of the trout: it spots a dragon-fly nymph chasing a tadpole and it wants the tadpole before the nymph can get it. This two-fly combination is so effective at times that it hardly seems worthwhile to consider any other. However, like the Walker's Killer, it is not good in cold water.

At dusk, the Taddy should be fished by itself in short very slow pulls, quite near to the surface. In this way the silhouette aspect of the fly is most advantageously revealed to the trout. The silhouette imitation of buzzer or sedge is thus more real, since these creatures move slowly in little 5 cm bursts of energy. The live buzzer pupae actually wriggle intensively in order to produce this movement. Unfortunately, that type of movement cannot be simulated.

The two-fly rig of Taddy and Walker's Killer should be fished deep in medium fast 30 cm pulls in day-time. The best areas to fish are around weed-beds.

Gold-Ribbed Hare's Ear Nymph

The best version of this is the American pattern which incorporates black hackle fibres to simulate the wing cases. The smaller sizes simulate various ephemerid (may-fly) nymphs whereas the long-shank size 8 or 6 flies imitate very effectively the nymphs of damsel flies. The fly is quite deadly when fished properly, especially when may-flies or damsel flies are prevalent. Damsel flies, by the way, are those flimsy skinny dragon-flies, usually bright blue or olive green.

The may-fly nymphs are usually active free swimming types, dashing about from stone to stone, or from weed-bed to weed-bed. The gold-ribbed hare's ear should therefore be fished quite deep to imitate the stone-dwelling nymphs, or close to the surface near weed-beds to imitate the other. Retrieval should be in medium fast pulls (quite jerky) of 15 cm, with a short pause between pulls.

The situation is a little different when you try to simulate damsel nymphs. Just prior to hatching, they rise up to the surface from 2 m or more of water and swim steadily toward the shore where they climb up a reed stem to hatch. They should thus be fished on a floating line and retrieved slowly but steadily. 'Figure-of-eight' bunching is probably the best method of retrieving in this manner: the retrieved line is collected in 'figure-of-eight' coils in the hand. When you use a shooting-head, each coil should be dropped as it is collected. (Normally all the coils would be retained in the hand.)

Dawn and dusk are best for simulating may-fly nymphs, although they do hatch during day-time, and a hot blazing sun is best for damsel nymphs.

The Muddler Minnow

Some American and English fly fishermen refer to this as the 'Magic Minnow' and they are not far wrong. This is an American pattern designed to simulate the sculpin of North American and Canadian streams. The sculpin is a rather flat large-headed small fish, which lives among the stones in river-beds. It looks very much like a catlet, (a small catfish) quite common in South African waters. Trout, especially large trout, take it for the catlet. It is thus a good big fish fly. A fast deep retrieve (*i.e.* strip retrieve) is the way to fish this fly. It is especially good in still water near dam walls and old river-beds.

The Muddler has many other attributes. If greased and twitched across the surface, it gives a fine grasshopper imitation. If fished deep in short jerks, it will also be taken for a dragon-fly larva. It may also be greased and fished on a short (1 m) leader with a lead core line. In this case it should be a twitch retrieval, with pauses of five seconds each. This will cause it to move across the lake or river-bed like an injured minnow.

All this adds up to a very versatile fly which should be in every fly-box.

The Mickey Finn

This is the cold-water fly 'par excellence'. It is an 'attack' pattern: the fish seem to attack it rather than feed on it. It will often produce fish after a sudden temperature drop. In early or late season, when the water is permanently cold, this fly will consistently beat all others.

The Mickey Finn garbed in yellow and scarlet simulates nothing — it is simply an attractor. It should be fished deep and very fast. Fish will hit it very fiercely, so be prepared for 'smash' takes. Since it attracts large fish it pays to use a 4 kg point or stronger. For me, this fly has caught more early and late season big fish than any other in the box. In the United States it has accounted for many record fish.

The Invicta

This is one of the few traditional patterns which competes favourably with the modern flies of the last ten years. The Invicta comes very close to simulating a hatching sedge. It is therefore most effective in hatches of sufficient density to cause trout to rise. On these occasions it will beat all other patterns with ease. The living sedge pupae move very slowly in little wriggling slow-motion dashes. The Invicta should therefore be fished on a floating line just below the surface and in short very slow pulls.

Black Buzzer

'Buzzers' is the name given by anglers to the pupae and imagoes of the chironimid flies (non-biting midges). The larval form is the familiar blood-worm. The buzzer is a major diet ingredient of the still-water trout, possibly accounting for 50% of his protein intake during summer months. As a general rule, buzzers will hatch over 2 m or more of water, either in the early morning, or at dusk and the first two hours of darkness. Buzzers hatch in profusion on those soft warm summer evenings when the mosquitoes seem determined to suck you dry. There are many species in the buzzer family, but by dusk they are all represented by a black silhouette pattern. Ideally, you should use two buzzer flies on the leader, one of size 10 or 12 and the other size 8. This will cover most of the pupae sizes. If you have difficulty in casting at dusk, *i.e.* if you produce leader tangles, use the smaller buzzer only. During a buzzer hatch trout will eat nothing but buzzers, and only a buzzer imitation will fool them consistently.

Buzzers should be fished on a floating line, with the leader greased to within half a metre of the fly. The retrieval should be in very slow short pulls of 5 cm. Try to ascertain the path of the trout by watching the rises. Anticipate where the trout may be and cast just in front of him.

The Whisky Fly

This fly built a reputation for big rainbows in the U.K. It is a good all round lure and an effective all-season pattern. It works well in cold and warm water alike. It is particularly good on bright warm days if it is fished very deep and fast. It is purely an 'attractor' pattern and shows up very clearly in the water. It works well in muddy water. This fly is the best of all the patterns for trolling. Use a strong leader, for fish will hit this fly ferociously. The retrieval should be in fast long pulls.

Polystickle.

This is rather a special lure. It is not an attractor, but a fry imitation. It was developed by the British angler Dick Walker and works very well in South African waters. The polystickle will catch fish throughout the season, but this fly really comes into its own towards the end of the season when shoals of fry collect in the shallows. The trout will harass the small fish and feed on them extensively. Cast a polystickle into this activity and you are on to a sure thing. The trout will hit it almost as soon as you move it. It is particularly good for brown trout. The retrieval should imitate the movement of a small fish, *i.e.* short dashes of varying length with frequent changes of direction achieved by moving the rod tip.

The Black Marabou

The pattern I use is by Barry Kent. It has black marabou wings, scarlet marabou throat and a black body with silver rib. Jungle cock is added to the wing. This is a good fly, especially in late and early season when toward evening the sun has warmed the water over the shallows. It also works well in murky water. Fish it about 1 m down in fast long pulls and be prepared for 'smash' takes.

Well, that's my selection! Armed with these patterns you should catch fish under most conditions experienced during the season. Always remember though that the way in which you use a fly is usually more important than the pattern of the fly. All successful anglers know this: they are constantly concerned that their fly move in a natural manner. Remember, too, that we fish for the pure pleasure of the game. If you cease to enjoy it, stop for a while and relax. Treating the water as your enemy leads to frustration. Why not watch the little nymphs at the water's edge? See for yourself how they move and then apply the knowledge to your fishing.

Tadpoles and Porringe
By Bill Steele

It was a typical late November Belfast morning. The grey light of dawn was spreading softly across the sky trying vainly to penetrate the rolling shrouds of mist. A soft ripple lapped at the boat. The shucks of chironimid nymphs lay in inch-thick heaps of brown along the bank where the wind and waves had brought them. Here and there the white spot of vacant breathing tubes showed. Overhead the invisible hadedah ibis were calling as they winged their way to secret feeding grounds. A lone trout silently broke surface as it 'head and tailed' to a nymph just 3 m from the shore.

It looked as if a nymph imitation fished just under the surface would be the best technique. Accordingly, I tackled up with a floating line, a 2 kg point and a size 12 Gold-Ribbed Hare's Ear Nymph. Having made sure everything was shipshape and that my landing net was to hand in the boat, I headed for the weedy shallows at the far end of the lake. Experience had taught me that nymphing trout would be moving in heavier concentrations over the weed-beds. Not only had I seen a trout 'head and tail', but the weather conditions indicated this kind of feeding behaviour. The larger trout habitually patrolled in 30 m beats, casually sipping up nymphs as they struggled to emerge in the surface film. The pale sepia may-fly (ephemerid) nymphs would hatch for approximately an hour after dawn, (head for the surface in short jerky movements,) and metamorphosing into the dainty gossamer-winged duns which headed for the shore and safety. There they would wait until conditions were right before returning to lay their eggs and once more become prey for the trout as their spent spinner bodies lay dead on the water.

I carefully cast my fly at the fish and timed my rate of retrieval to simulate the nymph movement. When you fish for patrolling trout it is essential to study their movement and cast to an anticipated position where you hope they will be two or three seconds after the fly has landed.

I was on the fifth cast when the line moved in a short jerk away from me. I struck. The line straightened in a burst of fine spray and sizzled through my fingers as the fish headed for the nearest weedy refuge. I laid the rod over, applying side-strain to turn him. There was no response and I knew I was into a big one. Our dams hold some really big rainbows and I knew this one could break me with ease if it reached the weeds. I increased the pressure to maximum and watched in dismay as it surged across the remaining few yards and bow-waved into the weed-bed. The line went slack and the old 'lost a big one' feeling came over me.

With no time to lose, I replaced the point with a heavier 3 kg half-metre length of Platil Strong and tied on another Gold-Ribbed Hare's Ear. Half an hour later, with no more takes and surface activity ended, I put down my rod, rested and considered a new approach. The ephemera were no longer hatching and I reasoned that it was early enough for the trout still to be feeding. But on what? It would have to be sub-surface life of some kind and the chances were that the trout were picking some aquatic life form off the bottom. Possibly they would be hunting the edge of the weed-beds seeking nymph forms as they strayed into the open water. Since I did not know what to simulate, I tied on my general attractor nymph pattern the Porringe.

The porringe is a fly tied on to a size 10 to 14 long-shank hook, the rear half consisting of fluorescent orange and the forward half fluorescent pink floss, over which is wound a layer of PVC film. The fluorescent floss glows through the PVC, giving a life-like appearance to the body. It imitates nothing in particular, but everything in general, as regards body shape. The black silk head gives it the appearance of an insect and the bright colour works as

1 Muddler Minnow
   (SA pattern)
2 Black Marabou,
   designed by B.
   Kent
3 Whisky Fly (UK
   pattern)
4 Yellow Sweeny Tod
   (UK pattern)
5 Tadpole Muddler,
   designed by W.
   Steele
6 Killer Nymph,
   designed by W.
   Steele (deep-water
   fly)
7 Standard Polystickle
   (UK pattern)
8 Carp Polystickle,
   designed by W.
   Steele
9 Mickey Finn (USA
   pattern)
10 Texas Rose Muddler
11 Mrs Simpson
12 Rasputin (UK
   pattern, deep-water
   fly)
13 Brownie Boozer,
   designed by W.
   Steele
14 The Taddy,
   designed by W.
   Steele
15 Bead Micky,
   designed by W.
   Steele
16 Rainbow Toddler,
   designed by W.
   Steele (early
   season fly)
17 Feather Fibre
   Nymph
18 Black Corixid,
   designed by B.
   Kent
19 Gold Nymph

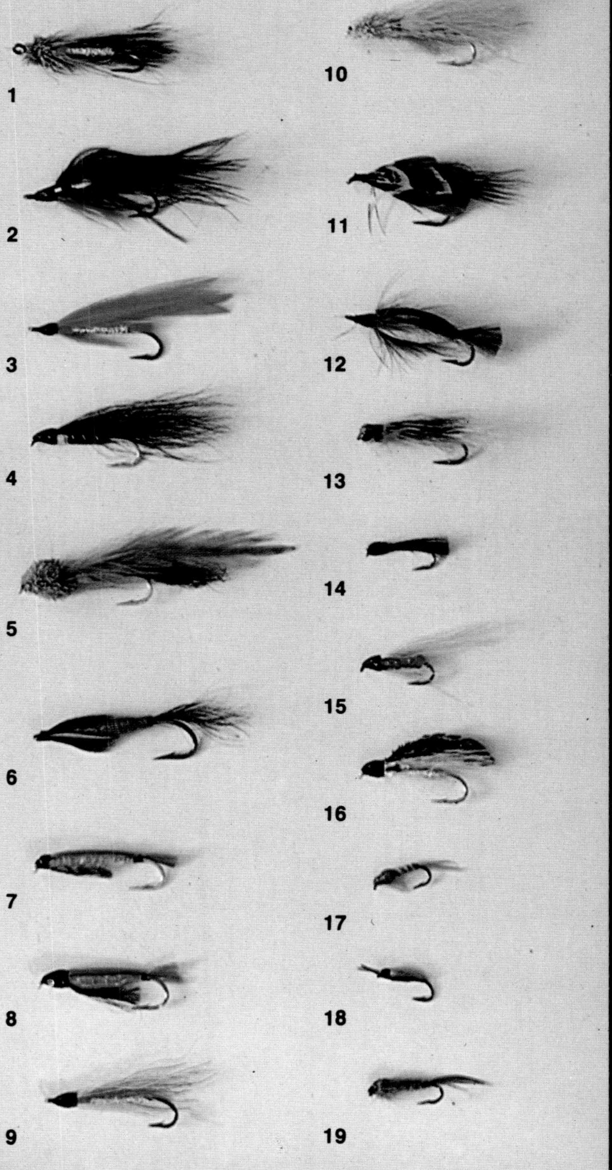

87

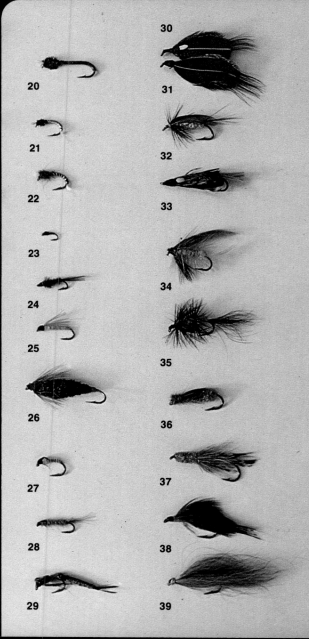

20 Giant Claret Buzzer
21 Olive Buzzer, designed by S. Stephens
22 Black Buzzer
23 Black Buzzer (standard UK pattern)
24 Steele's Nymph, designed by W. Steele
25 Porringe, designed by W. Steele
26 Stevie's Dragon, designed by S. Stephens (trolling fly)
27 Sedge Pupa, designed by W. Steele
28 Gold-Ribbed Hare's Ear (USA pattern)
29 Damsel Wiggle Fly Nymph, (USA pattern)
30 Walker's Killer with Jungle Cock
31 Walker's Killer
32 The Machadorp
33 Vlei Kurper by W. Steele
34 Invicta
35 Fuzzywuzzy (Blue Hackle)
36 Dragon-Fly Nymph
37 Muddler Minnow (USA pattern)
38 Hammil's Killer (New Zealand pattern)
39 The Scampy, designed by M. G. Salomon

an attractor. It has proven itself as a 'life-saver', frequently nailing fish when nothing else will.

I decided to fish the weedy edges and commenced double-haul casting. I worked my way around a weedy bay 40 m away. By now the sun was up and the water flat calm. In conditions like these 'fine and far off' is a good operating maxim. I had switched to my carbon-fibre rod, an AFTM 8 slow sinking shooting-head and 15 m tapered cast. The cast had been rubbed down with toothpaste to remove 'flash'. The fly was tied with a blood knot to a 1 m 3 kg Platil Strong point. My casting was operating smoothly on this day! I was able to drop the fly gently right at the weeds' edge. I counted to 60 and retrieved the fly in 10 cm jerks.

After about 20 minutes of fishing in this way I hooked and boated a 1 kg rainbow hen in fine condition. She had fought spectacularly, leaping prodigiously and trying with all her instinctive fury to rid herself of the sting in her mouth. The take had been ferociously sharp. She had obviously hit the porringe at full speed, which is usual with this fly. Fortunately the leader had survived the impact and finally exhausted, she had rolled, red and amethyst shining, into the net.

After killing the fish I spooned her in an attempt to ascertain the life form she had been feeding on. Spooning is a simple method of examining the stomach contents without gutting the fish. The instrument used is a marrow spoon, a long tapered spoon. This is inserted through the mouth and down into the stomach. By giving the spoon a full turn it can be withdrawn with the entire stomach contents. If these are placed in a small dish of water, they can easily be opened out and examined at leisure. Her stomach contents consisted of a few blood worms and masses of small tadpoles. The tadpoles had been whitened by her stomach acids but the eyes were still black. There was nothing in the fly-box to imitate a tadpole, however. With breakfast in mind I rowed back to shore and my caravan. Once there, I planned to break out my fly-tying kit and tie up some tadpole imitations.

I started by drawing a tadpole. It's silhouette determined the shape – all head with a small tail. The colour was easy, simply black. I finally came up with a suitable pattern, using black squirrel tail hair. The hair was tied forward on a size 10 hook and then bound down with black silk. I then varnished the silk lightly. I tied the hair all round the hook shank, not merely on top as in the case of most flies. Next, I pulled the hair back and tied it down halfway along the hook shank. When I did the tie-down halfway along the shank, I manipulated the hair so that at the front of the hook it bulged into the shape of a tadpole head. I then put three coats of varnish on the head shape, snipped the tail to the correct length and there it was – the Taddy, a tadpole imitation!

I made up half a dozen (they are very quick to tie and possibly the simplest pattern ever) and headed back to my anchorage.

Using the same technique, I cast to the weed's edge and began a slow short jerky retrieval. The fly had moved about 1 m when I was hit by a 'smash' take which broke the leader and numbed my wrist. The fish must have hit the tadpole fly at full speed, for the resultant shock had snapped the point like cotton! I changed to a 3 kg point and cast again.

Once more the take was instantaneous, but this time the leader held. Subconsciously, I had applied full side-strain and the fish headed for the open water in a long run which stripped off 30 m of the shooting line flat monofil. He fought hard, slugging it out under the surface, never once leaping. Eventually he came to the boat, made one last dash for the weeds and slid into the net. He was hook-jawed, suffused with crimson, shining silver and fat. He weighed 2 kg exactly and was in beautiful condition. I measured him and slid him back to his own element: One day he would weigh much more and maybe we would meet again.

I went on to take my limit in the next half-hour. Obviously, the new fly was a killer. On many trips since that one memorable morning the taddy has given me limit bags. There is evidence to suggest that trout also take it as a chironimid imitation. It works well when these flies (buzzers as fly-fisherman call them) hatch in profusion in the evening.

The porringe and the taddy are two deadly flies which are never missing from my fly-box. It seems almost unfair on the trout, but then trout appear to get to know flies over the years!

Deep-water fly-fishing
By Bill Steele

This is a much neglected aspect of trout fishing in South Africa. One of the reasons is the lack of deep water (8 m or more) in local trout dams. Another is the shortage of written works on the subject.

The greatest single problem is getting the fly down to these depths as quickly as possible. Even with standard fast sinking fly-lines this could take anything between five and ten minutes. Most anglers will not wait that long, so every cast is useless. Or, if they do wait, they quickly discover that most of the day is wasted in this way.

The answer to this problem is relatively simple, but it does require sound shooting-head casting skills. Long casts are an essential part of deep-water fly-fishing. It doesn't take much thought to appreciate that in a dam with a depth of 15 m or more, a 15 m cast means that the angler does nothing more than retrieve his line straight up. In fact, he won't be bottom-fishing in the true sense. Hence casts of 35 to 40 m are essential and these can only be achieved with the double-haul and shooting-head technique, discussed elsewhere in this book.

The fastest sinking fly-lines available on the market are either American lead dust-core lines or European copper-core lines. Neither of these are really good enough for our purpose, for which we need solid lead-core lines, and very soft lead-core lines at that. At the time of writing soft lead-core fly-lines have yet to appear in South Africa. Nevertheless, there is an answer and a very cheap one. This lies in the lead-core trolling lines used by the sea angler.

Trolling lines come in a variety of thicknesses and finishes, but one that is easily obtainable is ideal for our purpose. You require the lightest trolling line you can get and it should be covered with a braided nylon which, in turn is covered with a plastic film. It is normally purchased in 100 m reels.

Cut off 8 m of trolling line and nail-knot 0,6 m of 7 kg nylon to one end. Nail-knot the other end to your shooting line. Your lead-core shooting-head is now ready. This basic shooting-head can be made up in a more sophisticated fashion, giving better turnover and casting characteristics. To do this, splice 1 m of ordinary fast sinking fly-line to the leader end of the shooting-head, then nail-knot the leader to this. The problem here is the 'head-to-fast-sink' splice. This needs to be quite smooth. This can be done with a silk over-whip and a coating of pliable vinyl varnish.

To cast the new fast sinking shooting-head, the rod will have to be at least AFTM 9 rating and preferably AFTM 10. Carbon-fibre rods designed at AFTM 9/10 meet this requirement very well. Carbon fibre, unlike glass-fibre, is far more tolerant of line weight variations.

Casting the heavy shooting-head will require a much faster action on your part, plus a high level of skill. At this point I must warn the fly-rodder that a lead-core shooting-head can be very dangerous at high speed. I have friends with scars to prove it. Please be sure that you are well versed in the double-haul technique in all wind conditions prior to attempting the lead-core shooting-head.

Once you have mastered casting the new line, you will be amazed how far it will go with a following wind. Herein lies a further problem. Owing to the speed and length of shooting line you must be absolutely sure that the shooting line is not twisted or kinked but in perfect condition. Stretching the line prior to fishing helps a lot. The other point to bear in mind is the reel. Buy a large centre-pin of light construction (10 to 12 cm drum diameter). This largely eliminates the small 'line coil' problem.

Having established our new tackle we can now look forward to sinking times of one to two minutes, plus the added advantage of long casting potential. All that remains is to look at techniques and flies.

A short leader of about 2 m is adequate. It should be strong (breaking strain 4 kg), since this is a big fish technique and we have no desire to be broken. Additionally, the leader should be dyed dark brown to merge with the bottom. The dying is easily achieved by soaking the line in cold 10 per cent silver nitrate solution and exposing it to light.

Prior to selecting fly patterns we must first consider the type of bottom. If it is covered in snags we will have to use weedless flies, e.g. keel-hook flies. The keel-hook fly is relatively snag-free, although you will still lose them occasionally. On the other hand, its shape gives it very poor penetrating power. Keel-hook flies must therefore be very sharp and struck home very hard. An alternative is the lead-back fly. Unfortunately, these are not yet obtainable commercially. They are tied with lead wire along the back of the hook shank. Since this makes the fly swim upside-down, the body, wings, etc., must be tied upside-down.

Among the best patterns are Muddler Minnows, Polystickles, Rasputins, Whisky Flies, and any red/white hair-wing lure. At times nymphs may be successful, but in 90% of fishing outings the large lures bring most success. Size four flies are not too large for this kind of fishing, but size two is possibly better.

Standard fly

Keel-hook fly

Lead-back fly

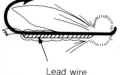

Lead wire

Having cast out and allowed the shooting-head to sink, don't forget that the fly may take another 30 seconds to reach the bottom. This is very important since the fish are normally right on the bottom.

In my experience the most successful retrieval is in fast long (arm-length) pulls with 3 or 4 seconds rest after each pull. This makes the fly behave like a small darting fish. Strikes are normally incredibly ferocious and it is very easy to be broken. The trout will often weave along behind the fly for some yards before attacking. When they do attack it is done at full speed. So, always try to keep the rod at right angles to the line; the rod will then absorb most of the shock.

Most of these deep-water trout feed on fish and dragon-fly nymph, but some of the deep-water brown trout turn to feeding on snails, leeches and crustacea. These are easily recognisable since they turn almost completely silver and the spots become black. These particular 'brownies' are possibly the greatest fighting trout of all, and well worth catching.

The fish-eating brown trout tend to establish territories from which they drive other brown trout. If you catch one you will probably have to move another 30 m to find another. Most of these will be big fish – 2,5 kg and over.

Not much is known about deep-water rainbows. They tend to shoal in small groups. If you catch one, it usually means there are others around, although the very big ones (4 kg and above) are normally solitary. One I saw caught at Dullstroom with this technique weighed 3,5 kg. It was taken with a size 2 Mickey Finn. In its stomach were two 5 cm dragon-fly nymphs, a 15 cm rainbow and a crab. This tends to confirm that big flies are most suitable. There are certain areas in any dam which tend to attract deep-water fish: old stream-beds, depressions or holes in the bottom, and rocky areas.

Often a fair idea of stream location or depth of water can be obtained by walking behind the dam wall and attempting to estimate what the valley looked like before the dam was built.

This kind of pre-knowledge can make quite a difference. It is a fact that in any deep-water location much of the bottom is barren of large fish, because there is no cover for the small fish and other creatures. The trout will only be where his food is! If you have a boat (and it may be used on your dam), you are in a fine position to explore the dam thoroughly with a plumb-line or, better still with an echo-sounding fish-finder. The information you gather in this way is invaluable.

Deep-water fly-fishing is in many ways an open door to big fish. I leave it to you to explore its possibilities and, I trust, to gain as much pleasure from it as I have.

The Dullstroom late evening rise
By Bill Steele

The sun had sunk below the blue-gums at the Dullstroom Dam a half-hour previously, and I was desperate. It looked like a blank day. It was late in the season and a sudden frost had put the fish down all day. Jim had had a take an hour or so before, and that had been the total reward for our efforts. Now, as dusk began creeping across the meadow, we were on the look-out for the late evening rise that is typical of that area. I spotted a number of rainbows rising in the shallow corner of the dam near the stream inlet, and carefully waded through the weeds toward them. It was almost dark as a large claret buzzer settled on my hand. I looked at it as its frail downy antennae sensed the wind for a scent of a mate. It was deep claret and approximately size 10.

Hurriedly I selected a claret buzzer imitation and greased my leader to within 0,3 m of the fly. I flicked it toward a fish rising 20 m away. Almost immediately I was into a stockfish which was quickly netted. Five minutes later I caught another. It was then that I heard it. It sounded like a deep slurp, invisible some 30 m away. Unlike the sipping rises of the stockies, this was the sound of a big fish feeding. With bated breath I double-hauled a long line toward the source of the big rise. I had retrieved about 2 m when I felt the tug and struck. The rod arched as the big fish tore off in a haze of spray. Within seconds the shooting-head backing was out as the fish bored for the old tree-stumps in the stream-bed. The reel was screaming as I applied side-strain – to no avail. This was a big trout and I could do nothing to turn it. All of a sudden the line went slack . . . it was gone. I comforted myself with the thought that I could not see in the dark and that the stream-bed was short. Well, at least I had two stockies.

I believe that fish was over 3,5 kg, a monster for Dullstroom. To this day I have never hit a Dullstroom trout that would not turn – with the exception of that one. The fly was one of the new 'buzzers' from Europe. It had always been extremely successful, hence the next article on how to tie and fish the 'buzzer'.

Buzzer-bashing for the fly-tier

Buzzer is the group name given by many trout fishermen to the various species of chironomid midges which abound in our trout waters. The chironomids or non-biting midges are an important part of the trout's diet. There are many species, varying very much in size and colour – black, brown, orange, red, green and golden-olive – from hook sizes 18 up to 6. A life-like imitation of the buzzer pupa can be a deadly fly indeed. They will catch fish at all times, but are especially effective during a buzzer hatch when a correctly matched imitation, i.e. one that approximates the colour of the emergent insect, will catch fish when all other flies will be completely ignored.

The history of buzzer imitations is fraught with unsuccessful attempts to imitate the midge pupa. Almost certainly the first effective imitation to appear was the 'Footballer' devised by Geoffrey Bucknall of England. He used contrastingly dyed horse hair strands wound around the hook to represent the segmented body. The footballer was soon succeeded by the buzzer imitations tied up by another Englishman, Richard Walker. These were later developed and marketed by Steve Stephens. They are very good imitations covering a complete range of colours and sizes. Rayon floss is used for the body and various herls for the thorax. The breathing tubes are copied with white hackle fibres. The really important innovation, however, is the sparse lurex wind under the floss. The combination of floss (which is translucent when wet) and the lurex gives the fly an 'alive glow'. This increases the attractiveness of the fly to the trout. Segmentation

The live buzzer pupa

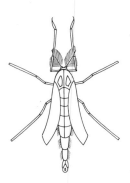

The live buzzer imago

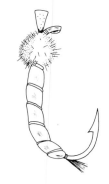

The buzzer imitation
Shown with sponge
forward breathing
tube

is achieved by spiral-winding a white or suitably dyed hackle stem over the body.

In almost every respect Stephens' buzzers are as near perfect as possible. Nevertheless, they have been improved in two further ways: the segmentation has been made more life-like, and the durability and whiteness of the breathing tubes has been increased. With the aid of modern PVC sheets, segmentation can be simulated most effectively. The trick is to find a fairly tough, completely transparent PVC or similar plastic material. This should be cut into 1,5-mm wide strips. One of these strips wound evenly up the body provides a remarkably life-like effect, increasingly so if the Stephens' body formula is maintained underneath it. For improved breathing tubes, simply substitute 8 strands of fluorescent white floss. Stephens recently incorporated a small wad of white polystyrene foam for breathing tube imitation. The advantage of this is that the fly attains the correct angle at the water surface, but its use is restricted as the fly becomes unsuitable for fishing in deeper waters.

The fly pattern is only half the battle. Correct movement, presentation and choosing the right location, are just as vital to success. Buzzers hatch in greatest density in water depth over 2 m or more. First, find water of this depth within casting range. Second, be there either at the crack of dawn or late dusk. An exception to this time rule are those days when rolling mist covers the dam. Buzzers hatch in these conditions, a fact which is important considering that the mist may last several days, especially around Belfast and Dullstroom.

Presentation can be a problem and the angler has to be reasonably sure at which depth the trout are taking the live buzzer pupae. Most of the time they will be just under the surface. The trout give themselves away by a characteristic 'head and tail rolling take' as they sip in the pupae. This generally happens in misty conditions and at dusk. At dawn they are far more likely to be near the bottom.

For surface fishing the leader should be greased to within 0,3 m of the fly. A long leader is preferable: 5 to 6 m is not too short.

The buzzer pupa moves very slowly in a succession of wriggling jerks with rests in between. The angler should, therefore, retrieve the fly in thumb-length twitches of the line with a five second pause after each twitch. It should take at least 10 minutes for a 25 m retrieval. Takes will be mostly gentle at or near the surface: the curve in the line between rod tip and water should be watched carefully for bite indications. You may expect 'smash' takes nearer the bottom, so be prepared holding the rod well up.

The buzzer should be matched with the hatching adult flies. They are easy to catch and it is well worth the trouble. Pick an imitation slightly lighter in colour and a little larger than the imago. The standard recipe for tying the buzzer is as follows:-

Hook:
6 to 16 extra short shank

Body:
1) Lurex under-rib
2) Rayon floss body

94

3) Hackle stem rib

4) PVC overwind

Thorax:

Herl (goose or peacock) or dubbed fur.

Breathing tubes:

1) rear: white fluorescent floss

2) forward: as above or white polystyrene sponge

1. Halfway round the hook-bend tie in a small bunch of fluorescent white rayon pointing rearwards. Tie in lurex for the under-rib, rayon body floss, hackle stem over-rib, and polythene strip.

2. Wind the silk to within ¼ hook-shank length of the eye.

3. In open turns wind —

(a) The under-rib to a point a ¼ hook-shank length away from the eye;

(b) Overwind with a single covering layer of rayon floss;

(c) Wind open turns of rib (silver lurex is easier than the hackle stem); then

(d) overwind with polythene.

4. Strip off excess materials.

5. Wind the silk to the eye and tie in the forward protruding white fluorescent floss for deep-fishing buzzers, or a small piece of white polystyrene sponge for floating buzzers. Wind the silk back to the commencement of the thorax.

Note. This operation imitates the forward breathing tubes which should be no longer than the hook barb.

6. Either dub the silk with mole or hare's ear (sizes 6 or 8) or tie in two strands of black goose herl (from primaries or shoulder feathers), using sizes 10 and smaller.

Note. Peacock herl can be substituted for goose herl.

7. Wind on the thorax and tie off.

Try dropping your buzzer into a glass of water. After 2 or 3 minutes you will see the under-rib glowing through the rayon body. I believe you will agree it is impressive. The under-rib technique can be applied to many wet flies. A whole new world of experimentation awaits the keen fly-tier. Try it on flies such as a green nymph, polystickle (in sizes 12 to 14), and sedge/longhorn nymphs.

Body silk	Under-rib lurex	Rib	Hook
Black	None	White	10
Black	None	White	16
Claret*	Red	White	10
Claret	Red	None	6
Pale olive	Green	White	8
Orange	Gold	None	12

*The best allround pattern.

Lady Grey
By G.P.G. Knipe

In March 1975 I was having a business discussion with a friend when I happened to mention trout fishing. Business was immediately forgotten while my friend gave me an animated account of an area called Lady Grey in the north-east Cape. I was soon convinced and in April that year was introduced to one of the finest trout waters that it has been my pleasure to fish. This assessment still holds good after five visits to the area.

The 1974-75 trout season had been a very memorable one for me as I had the good fortune to land many fine wild rainbows of over 2,5 kg. Only three of these fish were caught at Lady Grey, so what is it, you may wonder, that makes Lady Grey so memorable and exciting? I shall do my best to let you into the secret fascination Lady Grey has for the angler.

Lady Grey is situated some 60 km east of Aliwal North on the road to that other famous trout area, Barkly East. The only hotel in the Lady Grey area is the Mountain View, situated in the town itself. Holiday accommodation is being planned on Jack Isted's farm where an old farm house is sometimes available.

The river one fishes is the Karringmelkspruit and its tributaries which rise in the rugged Witberge, a spur of the Drakensberg. The soil of the area is made up of the black Drakensberg clay and basalt. This is important, as the soil stands up well to heavy rainfall and the river clears quickly after rain. Only small stock-farming is carried on to any degree and most of the area is covered with permanent pasturage. Rainfall is up to about 87 cm a year but can be as low as 50 cm on some farms in the district. About 65 per cent of the rainfall occurs between October and March. Snow can be expected from April and temperatures during winter are very low indeed.

On an average fishing day the water is cold and crystal clear. In the main one fishes fast runs and the deeper slower moving pools. The average fish is about 0,5 kg in weight, although in some areas the river has become over-stocked and 0,25 kg fish are more the order of the day. About one fish in fifteen is over 1 kg and my personal score shows that about one in 33 fish is over 1,5 kg. The best fish I have heard of being caught in the district was 2,7 kg, although it is my personal belief that a few fish of up to 3 kg do lurk somewhere in the 80 km of this delightful river.

These conditions would suggest a rod of between 2 m and 3 m in length and fly-lines of between number 5 and number 8. I have been most successful with a no. 7 wet line and with a no. 8 dry line. All this means, of course, is that my favourite rods balance to these lines and no other significance need be attached to this. I do believe, however, that a no. 7 wet line is important when fishing in turbulent water during the summer months.

The leaders I use are always between 3 m and 4 m in length and are balanced to the fly-line in use. Tippets range from 2 kg, to 3 kg breaking strain. I am sure ultra-light tippets would produce more strikes, but you would be broken more often than not as the fish are vigorous fighters.

Trout flies are a very personal thing with most anglers and I would not venture an opinion as to the best fly to use in the area. My experience has been that predominantly brown flies have been consistent 'good killers' for me, followed by black and green flies. Sizes range from nos. 12 to 6. Personally, I use nymph patterns whenever possible and these have brought me most of the success I have had.

Generally speaking, one should have warm heavy clothing for spring and autumn fishing and light clothing and waterproofs for the summer months. Since my adventure in the kloofs, (an account of which follows) I always include a 'space blanket' in my kit. Most fishing beats require a fair amount of walking so I carry only what is absolutely essential to the success of my day's fishing and my safety.

Talking of safety, my first visit to Lady Grey could easily have been my last fishing trip anywhere. Alf Fulford and I had an adventure which both of us will remember for the rest of our days.

On that beautiful April morning Alf and I decided to fish an area known locally as 'The Tunnel'. We were under the impression that we were involved in a 11 km walk and we calculated that we had time to cover the water and to do some fishing and arrive at the spot where our car had been left for us before nightfall. How wrong we were! Seven hours later Alf and I were indeed a sorry sight — both near exhaustion, Alf's waders torn to shreds and the boots badly holed. I was wet from head to foot, having tried to ford the river at a point where it was flowing at a tremendous rate. Night was closing in by the minute and we had no food, except two heavy bags of trout, no jerseys or warm clothing. We were dressed in thin shirts and jeans; we were in trouble and we knew it.

What saved us? Don't laugh, it's absolutely true. The dry right-hand corner of a wet box of matches and a piece of toilet paper! God knows what would have happened to Alf and myself on that freezing cold night without these two items which enabled us finally to get a fire going. Even with the fire it was still very cold and we shivered for several hours as we warmed first one side of our bodies and then the other, I had the added misery of drying my wet clothes piece by piece while I braved the chilly air in the nude.

The 'tunnel' is certainly worth a visit from all points of view. The fishing is good, the water interesting and intriguing. The scenery can only be described by all the well worn adjectives and clichés but it must always be borne in mind that this place is tough going and highly dangerous in places. In some places the going becomes very difficult and one is forced to resort to 'kloofing' to traverse some of the obstacles. Moreover, once you are in the kloof proper there is no way that you can climb out as the rock face is sheer. Severe rain storms are not unknown in the area. These factors together could create some very nasty situations for any unwary angler caught in the kloof. In one place there is a log almost a metre in diameter and about 7 m in length perched on top of two rocks at least 8 m high. This log was definitely not put there by people, and I am sure that I have no need to paint word pictures of the fate of anyone caught in a flood. The crafty vultures don't nest on the cliff face for nothing.

Without wishing to labour the point, I feel I must mention that a party of anglers who visited the 'tunnel' after Alf and myself were not as lucky as we were. They emerged with several injuries, including broken ribs. Unless you are really fit, experienced and have two days to spare, don't try to fish the whole of the 'tunnel'. The lower stretch of water holds excellent fish, as does the upper section; either of these can provide an excellent day's fishing without the risks involved in tackling the 'tunnel' in its entirety.

Our April 1975 trip was certainly unforgettable and exciting right up to the last minute of our stay. On the last morning Alf, myself and two other members of our party, Barry Kent and Dennis McCorkill, fished an area we christened 'the waterfalls' after two magnificent waterfalls found on this stretch of water. This is an easy stretch of water to fish and it holds some big fish but, like all big ones, they do not surrender to the first joker who passes by holding a fishing rod. Patience and stealth are needed, plus a fair share of good luck.

On the morning in question Barry and Dennis took up a position on a sandbank in the pool below the waterfall. Both had crawled there on their hands and knees and stayed down for fear of putting the fish down. Their foresight and skill was soon rewarded. Barry's fourth cast landed just to the left of where the main body of water enters the pool. Barry waited fifteen seconds and then started the slow retrieval of his Hare's Ear Nymph. After three pulls on the line it suddenly straightened and Barry had 1,75 kg of fury on the end of his line. Barry skilfully manoeuvred the fish into a back pocket of the pool, away from the fishing area and played it out.

Dennis was not to be outdone and kept dropping his William's Favourite into the area where the action was most likely to be. Half an hour went by before it happened. According to Barry who witnessed the scene, Dennis had just bounced his fly off the cliff face and waited for a few moments to meditate the mysteries of trout fishing, when he casually reached for his line and gave a gentle tug. To his amazement, his gentle tug was returned by a tremendous pull at the other end of the line. Dennis made a move to get up, but virtually fell back in disbelief as the water erupted in front of him, and a fish that looked all of 5 kg, took to the air. As the fish landed back in the water, Dennis was on his feet, with mouth open and knees shaking uncontrollably as the battle went back and forth across the pool. Dennis shouted instructions to Barry to have the net ready and not to make any mistakes when the moment arrived. Finally, much to Dennis's relief, the big rainbow tired and was netted by Barry, first time round. The fish tipped the scales at approximately 2 kg, being a little low on condition.

That morning I got two consolation prizes, two well conditioned 1 kg trout, caught a little way below where Dennis and Barry were fishing. Two and a half hours of fishing produced 6 kg of trout in four memorable fish.

These were the fish that landed up in our bags, but I always think that fishing stories should include at least one of 'the one that go away'. My encounters with big rainbows at Lady Grey have been many but one particular incident will live with me for many a long day. In January 1976 I managed to organise a few days' fishing at Lady Grey but on arrival I found the rain pouring down and conditions looking very poor indeed. Being a desperate type about my fishing, I determined not to let the heavy rain of the previous 48 hours dampen my enthusiasm, and got busy with rod and reel much to the amusement of the locals.

On that first afternoon I managed to hook and land a trout a fraction under 1,5 kg in the most appalling conditions, with the rain still pouring down and the river a raging torrent but reasonably clear. So I returned to the hotel somewhat wet, but feeling well satisfied with my efforts.

'Tiger' Stone was having a drink with brother Mike and in no time at all I managed to talk 'Tiger' and his son 'Bambi' into coming out with me the next day. How they must have regretted their brave decision as they drove back to their farm that night in heavy rain! It was a misty damp morning, heavily overcast, when we set out on our 35 km drive to the spot we were to fish. The roads we travelled were incredibly slippery and on three occasions I was convinced that we were not going to make it. We travelled in 'Tiger's' bakkie, locked in first gear for much of the time but even at these low speeds our vehicle was only just manageable.

At last, with much luck and many a hurried prayer, we arrived at our destination and walked down a steep koppie to a very interesting and beautiful stretch of water. The day had cleared a little and our enthusiasm soon returned. We fished through the morning session catching fish here and there. Just on lunch-time we arrived at a deep, long, fairly narrow pool that looked particularly intriguing, with a strong flow of water running through it. 'Bambi' had cast first and almost immediately was into a 1 kg, rainbow which he landed after a fight that took him 120 m down river. 'Tiger' and I fished the pool for some time before I had a heavy take but missed the strike. I quickly returned my fly to the water and did what I could to get the fly as deep as possible into the same spot. I had retrieved about half my line when I got a vicious take. This time I made no errors.

My rod doubled and down went the fish deeper and deeper into the pool, stripping line as it went. I knew it was a heavy fish, and he knew a thing or two about how to frustrate anglers. The battle lasted 30 seconds before my 3 kg breaking-strain tippet gave up the struggle and broke. This sequence was repeated no fewer than three times that afternoon and each time the leader either broke or was cut on a sharp ledge that ran across the pool. We never saw any of the fish except for the flash as they took the fly. What size? Your guess is as good as mine but they were big fish, make no mistake.

Like most trout streams, the Karringmelk has its legendary fish. He is known as 'King George' and has performed the most amazing feats. Breaking 5 kg, tippets like cotton and doing a 'Uri Geller' on a no. 6 hook was second nature to 'King George'. Perhaps we were mere mortals tangling with his majesty on that fateful afternoon. Would anyone catching a trout over a metre in length and sporting a crown, please return the Mickey Finn, Walker's Killer and Alexandria in its jaws to the writer? You may keep the crown.

The fly one uses at Lady Grey can be important, probably because of the crystal clear water. Let me illustrate this by relating an experience I shared with a fishing friend of mine, Gerry

Mulford. Gerry and I had three days' fishing at Lady Grey in April 1976. As we all know, that was a very wet month in most parts of the country. We battled for two days against the elements and had very little to show for our efforts. On the third day the weather cleared and we looked forward to some good fishing in the heavy water. Gerry had been having most of the success up to this point, with a battered William's Favourite. I had had a sudden inspiration on the first day that a Zulu would do the trick, but I had very little to show for my inspiration.

We started fishing and very soon Gerry had hooked a beautiful rainbow of about 1 kg. He played the fish well and the fight looked all over bar the netting. Indeed, I had unclipped my net ready to perform the act, but the fish had other ideas. Gerry started to give the fish some 'stick' to bring it to the net when it suddenly turned and ran towards him. In an instant it had turned and dashed back into the strong current in the centre of the stream and haired off. Gerry's light leader held for a while and then parted. He was upset about the loss of that particular fly as it had produced some good fish and most of the excitement in the previous two days. I vainly searched my fly-boxes for a fly that was a reasonably good replica of the battered one Gerry had lost but without success.

We fished on, but neither of us was having any luck. After two hours of fruitless fishing in a 2,40 km stretch of good water I knew something was wrong. We had fished a particular pool which simply had to hold a good head of fish, but we had not even a 'knock' to show for our trouble. I decided that now was the time to ditch my inspiration and try something new. Gerry was busy trying every William's Favourite in his box but could not find another that produced the results of the one he had lost. I settled on a Silver March Brown and the difference was quite incredible. My next six casts into the same pool produced five nice fish.

Inspired by these results, Gerry abandoned his search and also changed to a March Brown. He started to catch fish immediately. By the time we headed back to our car that night we had two full bags of fish which included several fine specimens of between 1 kg and 2 kg.

Is the moral of the story to use a Silver March Brown? No. I have had the same experience using other flies. In fact, I can think of an occasion where I had used five or six patterns with only meagre success, only to find that another angler fishing nearby had had a good day using a fly I had not considered (Muddler Minnow). Nymphs fished upstream have been the most consistent killers for me, but water conditions must be reasonably good to fish the nymph this way.

I hope these few incidents have given you some idea of the fishing and the character of the beautiful streams at Lady Grey, and that what I have written will give you some guidelines in planning your visit to the area.

The sound of a crystal clear trout stream in an area where the only other sounds are the unconcerned calls of the wild; a place where few men have been or are likely to go; no litter or other signs of civilisation to offend one's peace of mind. To me these are things of value. They also have a value to most of the brotherhood of men I know who take up the tapered line, fly, rod and reel to do battle with the noble trout. If your pleasure is in these things and you have the time, Lady Grey is an experience no trout angler should miss.

My introduction to Trout fishing in the Drakensberg
By Graham Barrett

The sound of the rushing waterfall was like music to my ears, and the cool crystal-clear water of the deep pool enchanting to my eyes. In such peaceful surroundings I had only one problem – my creel was still empty! I had finally made my pilgrimage to Underberg, trout fishing mecca of the Republic, but after two days I still had not caught a trout.

It was December, midsummer, when after much gentle persuasion my fiancée and I arrived in Underberg for a three-day fishing interlude before continuing on to Durban for our summer vacation. I had told my fiancée Anne, that the Drakensberg was on the way to Durban, and during the journey, I had to explain hurriedly that a two-hour deviation was well worth-while for a visit to a trout fisherman's paradise. So she had gracefully agreed to let me indulge in my hobby and passion, trout angling.

The country-side fully lived up to its reputation. The hills were green and rosy, willows gracefully draped along clear trickling streams and, most magnificent, the dark purple peaks of the Drakensberg loomed in the distance.

We had booked in at Dunraven Guest Farm for our stay, and took the turning to the left approximately 10 km before Underberg itself. The guest farm is a charming little set-up consisting of a farm house and a couple of rondavels. It is run by two very pleasant and hospitable hosts, Mr and Mrs Taylor, and the accommodation was most comfortable and very reasonable. The farm nestles amongst the hills and a stretch of the lower Umzimkulu River runs a scenic course for a couple of kilometres on the property. Before unpacking the car, I spent the remainder of the afternoon patiently exploring the pools and runs of this lovely river. The afternoon was hot, and the air was filled with many thousands of the white cabbage butterflies which are fairly common at that time of the year.

Rainy weather the previous day had left the waters rather muddy, but the river was still warm and there was no evidence of activity on the stretches which I covered expectantly with wet fly, nymph and streamer. I fished on till the sun set and left only after the last red flush of the dying day had departed from the skies and it was quite dark.

Disappointed, I returned to the farm for supper. At times like this one is filled with questions and doubts about flies, depths, techniques etc., but apparently the river had been fishing very poorly and no one had taken fish for days. There had not been much rain that season and the weather was hot without respite. A number of trout had been found dying on the banks.

The next morning I felt refreshed and decided that it was worth taking a drive and finding other waters which might be less affected by the unfavourable weather. Anne had spoken to some friends staying at the Sani Pass Hotel, and they had invited us there for lunch. I thought this a good opportunity to see more of the Drakensberg, to spend some time with Anne and, lastly, to wet my line in some new waters. The Sani Pass Hotel is built on the Umkimazana which rises below Hodson's Peaks and strung out from there are the Umkomaas, the Loteni and Insinga. These are brown-trout streams and as 'berg' streams, clear rapidly after a storm. I thought this a good venue for my next trout outing in the Drakensberg.

Over lunch I learned that there was a waterfall only 20 minutes walk from the hotel which runs into a few deep pools. It was in this direction that we set out with bellies full of food and wine, and hearts full of hope and excitement at the prospect of catching trout.

The waterfall turned out to be one of the most beautiful spots I have ever visited. The water dropped precipitously into a ravine 30 m below, splashing into a large emerald green pool. At first it did not seem possible to get down to the pool, but by walking a hundred or so metres further on, one is able to take a narrow path which winds down to the valley below and then walk back to the waterfall. The cliffs at this site are sheer. We made for a narrow shelf, where I assembled my tackle.

When one fishes waters for the first time, it is difficult to decide what fly is suitable. The usual dictates – dull weather and dark fly, and shiny flies for bright skies – are of some use, but there is a certain inner feeling, a sort of communication with one's surroundings that often decides which pattern is right for that particular time and place. I decided on a no. 8 Connemara Black and proceeded to cast along the near cliff to where the falling water churned the otherwise placid pool to a white froth. I was casting upstream and letting the current carry the fly back, retrieving just enough line to maintain adequate contact. Upstream fishing is quite different to casting down and across; often the only sign of the take is a hesitation in the line or the silvery flash as the trout takes the fly. Cast after cast failed to yield results; so I reeled in my line, sat on a rock and considered a change of strategy. The pool was roughly 40 m across and rather deep, which gave it an emerald tinge towards the centre and far wall. There was not much evidence of insect life, but on lifting a rock near the edge I briefly spied some nymphs. So I took from my fly-box a no. 10 Coch-y-Bondhu nymph which I tied myself, using copper wire as an underbody to give it weight. I tied this on to the extra light tippet I was using and cast up and across towards the deeper water of the far wall. I let the line sink, waited for a while, and then lifted the tip of the rod ever so slowly after the pattern of an emerging nymph. As I raised the rod, I felt a gentle nudge. I set my wrist back quickly, then thrilled to the vicious jerk which bent my rod and stripped line from the reel as the trout made a dash, then bore to the bottom of the pool. The rod was bent and quivering. Suddenly the fish took off again, this time rising to the surface and breaking the water with a spectacular leap and then down again, seeking to tangle the line on an obstacle and dislodge the hook.

The trout began to circle in the centre of the pool and gingerly I applied more pressure on the frail tippet, slowly bringing him closer. I could see the golden glint as the fish turned and pulled. He was tiring and soon, after some half-hearted splashing on the surface, he rolled on to his side. I led him over into the waiting net and lifted it to the bank. There he lay, my first trout of the Drakensberg, a beautiful orange and red-spotted brown trout just over 1 kg and in tiptop condition. My heart slowly stopped thumping and Anne, whose faith in my fishing ability was now restored, came over to admire my catch.

Using the same technique of weighted nymph, I was able to catch another brown trout of half a kilo before we had to return to the hotel where we informed the chef of the extra course for supper that night.

Although I have caught bigger and harder fighting trout before, this episode will always remain in my mind, partly because of the natural beauty of the setting, but more so because of the extreme delicacy and extra attention and thought required in successfully fishing that particular pool.

By 8.30 the next morning I was chatting to Mr Billy Hughes, club secretary of the Underberg-Himeville Trout Fishing Club (P.O. Box 7, Underberg 4590, Telephone 41). One can fish the club waters at a daily rate of R2,00 for rivers and R3,00 for dams, the annual fee being R22,00. For this small investment one has a choice of 200 km of river and many dams, each particular stretch of water being allocated by Mr Hughes on a first-come-first-served basis from 8.30 – 10.00 in the morning. I found Mr Hughes very friendly and helpful. He told me that owing to the lack of rain, the rivers were very low and fishing poor, and suggested I try a dam. Like most trout anglers, however, I have a strong preference for river fishing, and Mr Hughes generously offered to let me fish on his own farm, through which runs the Upper Umzimkulu. We decided to try this river and then continue on to the Drakensberg Gardens for lunch. I would recommend that the visiting angler make use of the facilities of the club, for one is assured not only of excellent angling waters at a very reasonable price, but also of expert and friendly advice on local fishing conditions.

The particular stretch of river recommended is opposite the trout hatchery run by the Natal Parks Board, where we browsed around before crossing the veld to the river. The grass was long, and colourful birds twittered to and fro amongst the branches of the trees. A large buck suddenly reared up not more than 10 m in front of us, thundered off into the distance, leaving us startled but thrilled to have seen such a magnificent beast at such close proximity. This is typical of the area which teems with wildlife.

As I had expected, the river was very low and the water crystal clear. There were, however, a few pools which looked fishable. I tied on a Muddler Minnow, a favourite fly of mine, with which I had had much success in the Eastern Transvaal earlier in the season. The beauty of the Muddler is that it can be fished both dry and wet and can be used in both dams and larger rivers. I have found that it is very effective when fished close to the surface during the evening rise on dams, but prefer fishing the fly deeper and even weighted in rivers. This river was running slowly, however, and the Muddler looked out of place in the clear shallow water. After a few fruitless casts I changed to a no. 10 Connemara Black and immediately felt more confident. The feeling of peace and contentment one experiences when fishing in such beautiful and untamed surroundings, totally isolated and removed from the hustle and bustle of the rest of humanity, is hard to describe. To me it is an integral part of the fishing experience, and one of the reasons why my angling has become more than a hobby and sport — a form of therapy which dispels the tensions and the worries that have become part and parcel of modern living.

I had become totally engrossed with my surroundings, and it was purely a reflex action when I set the fly in response to a sudden tug. The rainbow jumped out of the water almost immediately and charged downstream. After a brief but vigorous battle I landed the fish and was surprised to see it weighed less than a kilogram.

The Natal Parks, Fish and Game Preservation Board has been stocking rivers with a variety of rainbow trout equivalent to the Kamloops trout of the United States of America and Canada, which is renowned for its fighting ability, and I assumed this young rainbow was of that particular stock. I gently released the fish, continued fishing for a while but did not have any more takes.

After lunch at the Drakensberg Gardens Hotel we decided that it would be worth trying a dam that afternoon, and so set out for the Himeville Nature Reserve, 10 km or so from Underberg. The reserve has two dams, and on the larger of the two we launched a boat hired for a few rands. I began to row for the dam wall. It was blowing strongly and after five minutes I noticed that I had remained stationary relative to my car parked on the bank. Rather sheepishly I had to ask Anne to take the other oar, and after an energetic session of 'one-two-three, one-two-three' we reached our destination. The water adjacent to the dam wall was calmer, and I thought it a likely spot. I had instructed Anne in the rudiments of casting and gave her my spare rod. Together we fished, she with gay abandon, and I with caution, ducking occasionally as her fly whistled by close to my ear. After an hour of fruitless casting, she began to tire and insisted that there were no trout in the dam. A brief 'fight' with a clump of weed left her feeling more discouraged despite my confident prediction that we would have a bite at any moment. I was fishing with a home-tied Mrs Simpson. I carry a selection of patterns but I find it handy to have the same flies, some with lead-weighted underbodies and some without. Coloured nail polish on the eye is used to differentiate between the two types.

A weighted fly is preferable to lead shot as it makes for easier casting and a more natural presentation to the trout. A rise 15 m from the boat attracted my attention, and I cast to it. Almost as the fly touched the water there was a vicious jerk and the rod tip bent in an arc. The fish bore down and away from the boat, stripping line from the screeching reel. I could feel that this was a good fish and there was no stopping him in his initial determined run. Pumping gently, I regained a few metres of line, only to lose it as he took off again. Slowly he rose to the surface and my heart gave a leap when I saw the silvery outline briefly. Then he bore down once again, almost under the boat. The rod was almost doubled as I applied as much pressure as I thought the tippet could withstand. This to and fro battle continued until finally I brought the trout to the surface and he lay on his side alongside the boat. When I reached for my net, I realised that I had left it on the bank. Cautiously I reached for the trout but only succeeded in startling it so that it swam away and I had to bring it back. I took off my shirt and tried to wrap it around, but the fish stayed out of my grasp. By now the tension in the boat was such that Anne was close to tears and I was trembling at the thought of losing this fish. I had to stop Anne from reaching down and grabbing the fish. Finally I managed to hook my finger in its mouth and under the gills and lifted it into the boat where it lay, pink and silver, a rainbow cockfish of almost 1,5 kg in magnificent condition.

The wind increased in intensity. An ominous rumble and the grey thick mass of clouds gave warning of the approaching thunderstorm. By the time we arrived back at the farm it was pelting down and quite dark even though it was only six o'clock.

When we left for Durban the next morning it was still raining and the mountains were enshrouded with mist. It had only been a short visit to Underberg and the Drakensberg, but I had caught trout in a mountain stream, river and dam under a variety of fishing conditions, and felt enriched by the experience.

I would advise a prospective visitor to the area to time his trip early in the season or in autumn when the rains have cleared and the rivers are running clear and strong. Dam fishing, however, , remains good throughout the season.

Underberg and the adjoining Drakensberg offer the angler a choice of waters, from the dams with rainbows up to 5 kg, to the clear berg streams with their wily browns. The visiting angler will be well and truly hooked by the area's charm, hospitality and good fishing.

Jimmy Speedie proudly holds a 3,52 kg Rainbow Trout hen fish caught on a no 6 Hammil's Killer at the Belfast Angling Club's waters in the Eastern Transvaal

Dry-fly fishing
By
Royce Rosettenstein

Dry flies are designed to match a natural aquatic fly or an insect that has fallen into the water and is floating on the surface. Therefore, the artificial fly must resemble the natural fly as much as possible and the tie must be perfect. A good fly does not sit on its tail nor lean on its chin. The nearer to parallel the better, even though many natural flies are partially submerged.

The most common dry fly is the standard upright wing tie patterned after the common natural flies found on a stream. Many are tied with wings outstretched like a downed natural.

The other large Muddler type flies are designed to ride turbulent waters as at the head of a pool in cascading water. These big dry flies are designed to attract the big ones waiting for something substantial to come their way. Joe's Hopper is one of the most popular large flies, especially in local waters.

Every trout fisherman should stock his fly-box with a few basic proven flies. I would choose the following basic patterns: Mooi Moth, Black Flying Ant, Red Tag, Black Gnat, Blue Dun, Ginger Quill, March Brown and Coachman.

These basic necessities are bound to be useful somewhere, sometime. To have a well-equipped fly-box, one should have many more patterns of different sizes and designs.

Most anglers consider dry-fly fishing the most demanding method of fishing but it is nevertheless the best way for a beginner to start. In South Africa, however, we do not have the numerous hatches and conditions for the dry flyer. As our water temperatures are higher than elsewhere, the fish tend to lie on the bottom of the lake or river bed. Nevertheless, the dry fly is easier to cast than the wet. Also because the angler can see drag when it occurs and see the fish strike, he is able to set the hook more quickly.

The principle of dry-fly fishing is that the fly should come down the stream exactly like a downed natural. Therefore it is very important for the fly to be floating free on a natural drift. Sometimes the amount of drag can be so small as to fool a veteran but never too small to deceive a trout.

Without a natural drift, strikes will be few and far between. Sometimes trout rise so fast in the middle of a hatch that you think all you have to do is throw a fly on the surface and wait for a take. Then a trout comes up and gobbles a natural fly a few centimetres from your fly. That is when you begin to get the message! the fly is either going too fast or too slow or traversing the stream across current.

Drag is caused when the fly is pulled by the leader and line at a rate slower or faster than the current or cross-current. The fly should ride straight downstream like a natural fly at the mercy of the current.

When the rise is fast and furious, the angler tends to become excited and instead of bearing down on one fish, makes wild inaccurate casts. Regardless of how hard trout are feeding, your results will be very poor if you don't put the fly down the groove to a particular fish.

Like all rules, the free float theory has exceptions. For instance, in the eddy behind a protruding rock or log is a spot where a dry fly does not need to be floating dead centre in order to get a bite. In such an eddy even the natural fly does not float normally, but is pulled and whirled by the varying currents. For this reason, the trout lurking there will not be upset by a fly not floating free. In such a situation, the angler must wade in close and cast a short line, hold the rod as high as possible and try to have only the leader and fly on the surface. It is thus possible for the fly to whirl lightly around in the eddy which is sufficient for the strike. This same technique also pays off at the head of a pool where similar conditions, such as eddies and back currents prevail.

A beginner must always be alert while he is on the stream as the quickest way of getting on to trout habits is to watch them feed. In a clear stream one can get a close-up view of how trout take a fly. On their feeding stations they generally seem to see the fly about a metre above them, as it comes down the current. As it comes nearer, they rise a bit higher to meet it, and as it comes over them they drift back right under it to suck it in.

Cruising fish call for special treatment. A fly slipping along on the current does not always pay off. The fish that slam it hard if it happens to come across their path, are those which have left their feeding stations. They are on the make, out looking. You can see the 'vee' they cut as they swim just under the surface, and watch the water bulge as they grab a nymph just before it reaches the top. They take an erratic course across the pool, so that you must establish which way your fish is going, then quickly drop the fly about a metre in front of him. Generally he will spot the fly and take it immediately. Sometimes it helps to impart a jiggling motion to the fly with the rod tip, making the fly shiver and shake on the surface. Then let it sit quietly, give it another twitch, bring it slowly along the top to pick it up for the next cast. Trout may hit a fly during any of the above manoeuvres. They often hit when you are bringing the fly along the surface because they think it is a freshly hatched fly taxiing across, trying for elevation.

Most anglers fish far too rapidly: a few casts in one pool and then off to the next! One should spend plenty of time and caution when fishing a pool, especially when fish are rising.

The approach to a pool is more important than most anglers think. Before even starting to fish, the dry-fly man should study the pool or run carefully. Trout always lie facing upstream as they feed. Therefore, the logical approach in order not to be seen is from the tail of the pool. The beginner always seems to gravitate to the head of the pool and, once there, stands on the highest rock where all the trout can see him. Or he wades noisily out into the centre flushing trout from their feeding places.

If there are bushes, stand in front of them so that your movements will not be flashed against the sky. Walk softly so that vibrations will not be sent out to be picked up by the fish.

Fish out the bottom of the pool and work your way slowly up along it, fishing the various currents as you go. Often the trout in the pool will become accustomed to the angler and will break all around him.

Most dry-fly men don't get close enough to the fish. They try for long casts which end up in the fly being out of control. Get close to the fish, and keep the cast as short as possible.

7 Tiger fish

(Hydrocynus)

Tiger fish, like eel, are only to be found in rivers running eastwards. This fish, size for size, is the finest freshwater sporting fish in the world. You will be lucky to land three of every ten tiger fish that take your spoon or bait – the others will break the line or a swivel or twist the line around an obstruction.

Feeding habits

The tiger fish is a ferocious predator and when on the bite will attack anything moving that resembles its prey. Tiger fish eat fish of up to 1 kg or 1,5 kg in weight, a wide variety of insects, frogs, mice, – in fact, virtually anything that moves in the water and can be swallowed.

Breeding habits

Tiger fish spawn during spring and will spawn twice during a season if the water temperature rises sufficiently early in spring. The fish migrate up river and spawn in the shallows amongst aquatic growth.

Size hooks

Tiger fish have large mouths and a large hook (from a no. 1/0 to 6/0 shank) should be used with bait. If a spoon with only a single hook is used, the hook should extend the length of the spoon. Many lures designed for other species of fish are also suitable for tiger fish. The hooks must be changed, however. A tiger fish will easily crush a small treble hook in its bony mouth. Therefore, a single hook is recommended. Invariably, the clips connecting the hook to the lure are also unsuitable for tiger fishing and will be torn apart by the great pressure applied when the tiger strikes. Heavy-duty clips should be used.

Rod

Use a slightly heavier rod, sound enough to withstand the first terrific rush of a tiger fish. I prefer using a flexible rod when spinning from the side or drifting in a boat. If you are trolling, a slightly less flexible rod is more suitable. The rod must be capable of setting the hook in the fish's bony jaws when you strike. I have witnessed anglers using short boat rods suitable for tunny and large barracuda to catch tiger fish. Their reel resembles a winch, and if the luckless tiger cannot dislodge the hook with its first leap out of the water, it is speedily hauled into the boat.

Line

Many anglers use a line with a breaking strain of 14 kg or more. As the average tiger fish caught weighs from 3 to 4,5 kg, I feel such a line is a little heavy and prefer to use one of 3 to 6 kg breaking strain, although it is no disgrace to use a heavier line.

Trace

As tiger fish have large razor-sharp teeth which will cut through nylon line instantly, it is essential to use steel wire trace. Ready-made traces can be bought but these are usually not designed for tiger fishing; the clips are too weak and the line too short. A trace of 60 to 90 cm should be made from steel wire of about 11 kg breaking strain. If the trace is too heavy you will not get many strikes. Tiger fish have no trouble in smashing the line with their tails if a shorter trace is used. Heavy clips and swivels should be used to connect the lure and the line. Avoid using bright brass swivels and clips as these attract small tiger fish which grab at them and cut the line.

Cut the required length of trace and slip on two sleeves of a suitable size. Thread one end of the trace through the eye of the hook (or swivel on the lure) around the shank and back through the eye. Slide one sleeve up towards the eye and over the end of the trace. Squeeze the sleeve in two or three places with a pair of side-cutters and cut off the end of trace protruding from the sleeve. Thread the other end of the trace through a swivel and repeat the process.

Bait
Strip Bait

The larger specimens are usually taken on strip bait. Fillets of barbel, yellow-fish and even tiger fish are the best bait, but any fresh fish may be used. The fillets should be about 12 cm long and 2,4 cm wide and should be threaded on to the hook in such a way that a small tail is left. The top end of the fillet should be securely tied to the eye of the hook. No sinker should be used. A float (not coloured red) may also be used to support the bait. Strip bait may also be trolled like a spinner.

Spinners

Tiger fish are usually caught with a spoon cast from a bank or trolled behind a boat, which must travel at the same pace at which an angler would retrieve the spoon when spinning. If the boat travels too fast, the angler will have far fewer strikes. If no results are obtained, try spinning a little deeper by placing some shot on the trace near the spinner. The best spoons are either plain, coppery, or silver or combined with red. The red colouring resembles blood which excites the tiger fish. A piece of red cloth

The Tiger Fish's powerful jaw and vicious teeth can easily mutilate a clumsy angler's fingers

or wool attached to a plain spoon often improves results. The spoon should be between 5 and 12 cm long. When tiger fish are on the bite, they will strike any metal-coloured object that moves. In fact, the curled top of a sardine tin with a hook attached to it has been used successfully when the angler ran out of lures and had nothing else available.

Choosing a suitable spot

When using fish bait, cast the bait into rough water and allow the current to carry it into deep calm water, or select a site where the river flows over a sand-bank into a deep pool. The mouth of a backwater is also a good spot, as is the base of rapids.

Anglers trolling from a boat have the advantage of trying the whole river, but they should remember to keep to the deeper water. The angler should always remember that wherever tiger fish are, their inseparable chums, the hippo and crocodile, are bound to be. The angler fishing from the bank should always have a long-handled gaff handy to avoid having to walk close to or into the water.

Striking and landing a tiger fish

The head of the tiger fish is hard and bony and the razor-sharp teeth interlock. The fish takes the bait or spinner with a terrific tug and should be struck hard as it starts its mad rush. When fishing with bait on the bottom, leave a metre or two of slack in the line so that the fish can swallow the bait and be hooked in the throat by the time it has taken out the slack. It also prevents the fish from pulling the rod into the water with its first wild rush. The drag should be carefully set to a minimum of resistance, as the power of a tiger fish taking a bait, particularly a moving spoon, must be experienced to be appreciated. Once hooked, the fish usually jumps out of the water and leaps into the air. There is little to beat the thrilling sight of a silvery-orange tiger fish dancing on its tail and shaking its head vigorously in an endeavour to shake out the spoon — which it usually does. The fish shakes the spoon so vigorously that you can often hear it rattle against its teeth. If the writhing and shaking is not enough to rid the fish of the spoon, it tries different tactics. One of its favourite tricks is to dash right up to the feet of the angler and then out again. As you cannot wind in the slack line as quickly as the fish swims, it will twist and dive and jump again and wind the line around the nearest object, even an overhanging branch, and break away. When the tiger fish is about to jump, the angler will see his line rising towards the surface of the water. He should be ready to swing his rod around to the side, pulling the fish as it jumps out of the water and taking in as much as possible of the slack line to prevent it shaking the hook loose. The angler must wind furiously to prevent giving the fish slack line. Remember not to keep your rod parallel to the water when playing a fish. Keep your rod upright. The fish is beaten by the play in the rod. When the fish runs, allow it to run. If it jumps, repeat the action of pulling the rod sideways until the fish is tired out.

Whilst on my last fishing expedition to the Zambezi River, I hooked a large tiger fish. Although the drag was correctly adjusted, the violent take broke my recently purchased line. (I later found the line was rotten.) The spoon remained lodged in the fish's jaws, however, and every 15 seconds or so it jumped out of the water in the same spot and unsuccessfully tried to shake out the hook. The fish's efforts to dislodge the hook became weaker and weaker, and after eight or nine attempts it jumped no more. Some 30 minutes later it floated to the surface, having drowned because it could not close its mouth. A sharp-eyed fish-eagle spotted it and although it weighed little more than the fish, managed to fly with it to a nearby sand-bank where it proceeded to tear it to pieces.

The fisherman who does not use pliers or carefully work the hook out of the tiger fish's mouth will make that mistake only once, as the fish can bite through the flesh of a human finger to the bone. One tiger fish I caught had bitten the spoon so hard that one of its teeth was actually embedded in the metal. Many a tiger fish has had to be sent to a 'dentist' for a broken tooth or two to be replaced before it was mounted.

Tigers and flies

The lone waterbuck looked up with soft eyes as the 4-m boat chugged by. The oily wake of the Zambezi spread in a continuous 'vee' behind us, softly caressing the lush marsh grass which grew in green carpets along the bank. A fish-eagle screeched from its watch-point around the bend of the river. A group of hippos, visible only by their nostrils and humpy eyes, defensively turned through the water studying the strange noisy intruder. The crocodiles basked in the morning sun, slowly digesting meals of long-whiskered barbel. The setting was an angler's dream come true.

We were headed upstream toward an island a few kilometres below the Deka rapids. We had planned this fly-fishing trip for tiger fish some months before in Johannesburg. Long discussions over midnight coffee on tactics and tackle were about to be put to the test. With almost no information readily available on fly-fishing for large tigers, we were very much in a pioneering position. We had to reckon with both the incredible power of the tiger and its fearsome razor-edged teeth. We had had much experience with trout and were familiar with salt-water fly-fishing at St Lucia. It was from the latter area that we pooled the knowledge upon which we based our campaign against the tiger.

We had each landed queen-fish and salmon weighing up to 7 kg on fly-rods, and we well knew that a standard trout fishing outfit was not up to the power and speed of these fish. We also knew that, if anything, the tiger was not only faster, but far more acrobatic . . . and then there were those teeth!

We had imported from Hardy in England some blanks which had been designed for European barbel. These are fast hard-fighting cyprinoids, not catfish. The blanks had a test curve of half a kilogram and an action which extended right into the butt. The rods were fitted up with the best rings we could find and a handle of the fly-rod type was built on with sheet cork and a screw-lock reel fitting. The reels were of the Seldex centre-pin type fitted with extra strong ratchet springs. We had decided to go for the shooting-head technique, not only for the advantages of distance casting, but also because we knew that the inertia of a sunken shooting-head would help drive home the hook.

The shooting-heads were AFTM lead-cored and nail-knotted to 300 m of 12 kg cobra flattened monofil. The flies were tied on 0/5 Salmon irons of best quality, carefully filed to needle-sharpness for good penetration as the tiger fish has a bone-hard jaw. Patterns were of three types only – a Mickey Finn for general use, a Parmachene Belle for deep water and a plain black fly for surface fishing.

The red and yellow Mickey Finn is universally regarded as one of the great attractor flies. For reasons not clearly understood it drives the fish to attack it, as opposed to eating it. The red and white Parmachene shows up as white and grey in deep water and can be seen by the fish both from above and below. The black fly shows up best at dusk. Pulled across the surface from below it can be clearly seen in silhouette.

All the flies were tied up from buck-tail. They were tied sparse for underwater action. Leaders were 3 kg with a 15 cm point of 3 kg stranded steel trace.

As the boat glided up-river we tackled up under the jaundiced eye of our Black guide. He simply couldn't believe that we seriously thought we would catch tiger fish with those thin sticks. Normally, his customers trolled with great silver spinners and short stout rods and a line with a breaking strain of 15 kg. Not only that, but his customers wanted to fish from land. Nevertheless, he was happy. While we fished for tigers he would fish for chessa, which was much better than toiling up and down the Deka rapids all day.

The boat nosed into a soft sandy beach pot-marked with the huge tracks of the previous night's browsing hippos. Charaxid butterflies zoomed to and fro, carefully avoiding the equally fast bright scarlet dragon-flies. Small yellow flowers nodded in profusion as a flock of busy egrets took off in a bustle of white. A glistening cormorant flapped his semi-dry wings and took off for the far bank.

We quickly surveyed the island – no crocodiles, no snakes, little rocky headlands and deep fast water. It looked good.

Our guide Joshua made for a shallow run and chessa. We took up stations on the rocks. The sun beat down and we commenced casting.

John was first. The water exploded with fury as the first tiger hit the big red and yellow Mickey Finn. We watched in amazement as the enraged fish performed every manoeuvre in the book. It looked quite small, but put up a performance to shame a big rainbow. It leapt, tail-walked, shook its head, made sizzling runs and bored deep. John handled it all with his usual skill, but his face was a mask of disbelief. For weeks after the trip he was heard to mumble 'impossible, impossible' at odd times. The electrifying performance of the first tiger finally ended. With all its energy resources finally burnt out, the fish slid quietly to the net. It weighed a little more than 1 kg and we were after fish of 10 kg. Tackle was hurriedly re-examined. We still believed it could do it, but were a little worried when we observed John tie on a new fly. 'Chewed to bits' he said, 'I think the steel trace is all right, but all the nylon covering has been stripped!' Nevertheless, we were back on the rocks at a speed which would have done justice to a klipspringer. We commenced casting.

I had decided to try the deep water at the end of a fast shallow run-off. I was casting to maximum distance, allowing the line to sink well down and retrieving in short jerks. My fly was a red and white Parmachene. On the third cast it happened. I had struck and the backing line was disappearing at tremendous speed. The reel check was screaming as a fine rainbow spray cascaded from the line. The hidden tiger was coming up to leap.

It burst two metres into the air, head shaking and the click of its grinding teeth clearly audible as it bit at the stinging fly.

It crashed back into the water, made another long run downstream and leapt magnificently into the air. By now it was 80 m away and still heading out into the river. 'That's not a fish, it's a damn crocodile' John said. 'Must have a 50 horse-power out-board in its tail,' Larry remarked. It was my turn to wear the mask of disbelief. It was now tail-walking 100 m away, its teeth flashing like sabres as it shook its head ferociously. So far I had only given line and not gained a single inch on my adversary.

Still it made dazzling runs and powerful leaps. I started to apply pressure—too early. The enraged tiger simply tore off more line and commenced another series of aerial acrobatics. Five minutes later the tables were turned. The fish was boring deep, still making vicious runs, but allowing me to recover line after every run. I prayed that it would not run toward me. I knew I would never keep up if it did. The hook would probably fall out of that hard bony mouth. Slowly I began to gain line by 'pumping' with the rod, i.e. winding and at the same time steadily lowering the rod and then lifting and heaving with it. It is a good method of moving a large fish. The fish began to move easily. Just like John's first tiger, it came quite easily to the big net once its energy was gone.

It looked enormous, shot with blue, green and orange, the great teeth still gnashing at the fly. John lifted it from the net with a thumb and finger grip behind the gills. He wore a stout gardening glove for protection. In the next instant the fish flipped, John's grip loosened and in seconds he was bleeding profusely from the left knee. The fish's teeth had lacerated his flesh. We quickly applied mercurochrome. He still wears the scar. It certainly drove home the lesson that you cannot be too careful with the tiger fish.

We weighed the fish. It was 7,2 kg, not enormous by any means, but it will never be forgotten. We returned the fish to the water! The tigers at the Deka area of the Zambezi are fished very hard. Most people kill all they take (20 or more a day). We wanted no part of this slaughter and felt that we were obliged to return our fish and do our small part to conserve what is probably the finest freshwater fishing anywhere in the world.

Over the next four days we caught and returned 156 tiger fish. None was bigger than 7,2 kg, but everyone tested our tackle and skills to the utmost. Weight for weight, the tiger fish easily was the finest fighting fish we had ever met. Our carefully prepared tactics had paid off, and for anyone wishing to experience the epitome of sport fishing and to return home weary but with a sense of utter contentment, I strongly recommend fly-fishing for the king of fish — the tiger.

October 1976 once again found Stan Lewis, Eric Weinstein, Peter le Roux, David Kahn and myself in the Senyati Gorge at Kariba, this time armed with a rifle as well as fishing rods. The humidity in the gorge had been building up for a few days and was almost unbearable, but the tiger fish loved it: wherever we looked we saw tiger fish jumping out of the water. By midday we had caught our fill of tiger fish averaging about 4 kg. They had readily taken spoons, fish fillets, the conventional Vuru-vuru spinners and even bright red and black trout flies with silver tinsel ribbing. It was unusual to catch tigers on fly in the lake itself, but previously I had had great success in catching tiger with trout flies in the fast flowing water below rapids. Eric hooked the two biggest tigers, both in the region of 7 kg. Despite our 'advice' to keep his rod up and not to fall out of the boat, he lost both fish the very first time they leaped out of the water. They had managed to find enough slack line to throw the spoon out of their mouths.

We noticed a waterfall running down the mountainside and pouring into a nearby creek. In an effort to find some relief from the sun, we tied the boat to a shady tree near the waterfall. The gurgle of the running water and the spray soon revived us and we took out our small bream rods and tied fixed-sinker no. 8 hooks on to a short trace and threaded on earthworms, ensuring that the point of the hook was covered. We started fishing for chessa on the bottom in some 10 m of water. My sinker had no sooner hit the bottom than I felt a fierce bite and struck. My rod bent under the weight of this smallish fish and there was much mirth from Stan and Eric when I pulled up a squeaker (klip catfish), locally known as 'crocodile killers' because of the spiky back fin which usually proves fatal to a crocodile foolish enough to eat one, as it lodges in its throat. The crocodiles in the gorge were obviously wary of this danger. At night, in the light of a torch one could see their evil non-blinking red eyes staring at one, but during the day they were seldom to be seen.

Several squeakers later I suddenly hooked my first chessa, so large that I could not control it with the light tackle I was using. A split second later it had wrapped and broken my line around an underwater tree-stump. Within the next hour we had lost a dozen chessa which had again speedily found an underwater obstruction, but after a tremendous battle had managed to land 4 of about 2 kg each. These fish have very small mouths but, weight for weight, are more powerful fighters than tiger fish.

Stan was watching the whirlpools formed by the water pouring into the creek and said that this was the type of terrain which bottle-nose loved. The water depth was just right and he changed his tackle, tying on a fixed sinker, a long-shank no. 6 hook and 2 traces about 15 cm long and the same distance apart. The bottle-nose is so called because its mouth resembles a mineral water bottle. It will slowly suck bait consisting of a clump of earthworms into its mouth and one should not strike when one feels the first slight pulling action on one's line. Rather wait until the fish has slowly sucked the entire bait and hook into its mouth and then give a more determined pull as it starts to swim off.

Stan's understanding of the water was right. He soon shouted that he had a bite and a few minutes later pulled in a 6 kg bottle-nose. We all changed our tackle and each caught several of these fish weighing from 4 kg to 7 kg. They are very oily, but make good eating if grilled and the excess fat cooked away.

The next day we headed for Fothergill Island, where over the years we had always caught our best tiger fish. During the first hour, however, not one of us even had a strike. We tried using spinners of all shapes, sizes and colours, but even a spinner which in the past had given me the best results, failed to do the trick. I made this spinner with piano wire, a small rotating blade, some red beads, a small lead weight and a no. 2 hook fixed below the spinner. A very small fish fillet (preferably chessa or bream, but tiger fillet will also do), must be securely tied to the eye of the hook, preferably with a piece of red wool, the one end of which should be cut to the same length as the fillet and left hanging alongside it. The fillet should be cut to the width and length of your small finger, and the rig should be made up as follows:

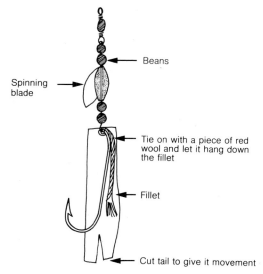

Beans

Spinning blade

Tie on with a piece of red wool and let it hang down the fillet

Fillet

Cut tail to give it movement

The secret of the success of this rig is keeping the spinning blade and the fillet small. Also, the spinner must be retrieved just fast enough to make the blade spin. I have found that if the rig is retrieved just a shade too fast, the percentage of strikes will be drastically reduced. With the introduction of Kapenta (sardines) into the lake, the feeding habits of the tiger fish have changed remarkably and the larger tiger will no longer take a spoon.

We moved from spot to spot without success and were convinced that we must have caught all the tiger fish in the lake the previous day. We approached a bay and noticed the shallow water boiling with fish and decided that it was time to relax after the rigours of a couple of hours of non-stop casting for tiger and to catch some bream for lunch. We could see the back fins of the larger bream cutting through the shallow water. We cast only a few feet away from the boat. We were each fishing with a fixed sinker with a no. 6 hook tied onto a short trace a few inches above it and another short trace with a second hook a few inches above that. No sooner had the bait reached the bottom than we felt a bite. Bream bite gently and must be struck. Without really waiting for a bite, we were striking and almost instantly hooking bream, often two at a time. This is the type of bream fishing Kariba used to be famous for, and we were fortunate to find a shoal of bream trapped in the bay by a school of tiger fish. I stopped to admire the beauty of Kariba. There was no sign of another human being, and the silence was broken only by the occasional cries from a pair of fish-eagles perched on the branch of a lone dead tree protruding from the water. A cormorant fearlessly dived into the shallow water a hand's throw away from us and, having caught its fish, perched on a branch where it spread its wings and sat motionless in the sun. A lone hippopotamus submerged half a kilometre away and we apprehensively kept one eye on it in case it took exception to our presence as it could easily have capsized our 4 m fishing boat.

The author with two Tiger Fish weighing 5,84 kg and 6,25 kg caught on a fly and a trout rod off Spurwing Island, Kariba

The deeper water behind the boat was shaded by a bank of oxygen weed about a metre below the water's surface. Out of the corner of my eye I saw the blur of a large fish and turned just in time to see a tiger fish of about 5 kg seize and bite a 1 kg bream in half. The fish saw me move and was gone in a flash, fearfully leaving the rest of the bream behind. It is by no means uncommon to catch a bream whose tail has been removed by a marauding tiger.

I now knew there were tiger fish to be caught, if only one knew how. I decided to present a natural bait to the tiger. I tied a single large hook on to a piece of trace, hooked a small bream through the jaws cut off its back fin, and, using no weight, cast it out into the deeper water. The tiddler could not have sunk more than a metre when there was a violent take. I struck hard and twice to ensure that the hook was set. My reel sang joyfully as the fish ran for several metres and then tail-walked along the water. The Black driver of our boat suddenly came to life and gave the traditional shout ('Tiiiger') in time to the melancholy cries of the disdainful fish-eagles. I had lost many tiger fish in the past and knew that the line was lifting through the water because the fish had finished its first frenzied run and was leaping to the surface. I was ready and as the fish sprang out of the water I swung my flexible trout rod as far back as I could. Try as it may the fish could not force any slack line and the action of the rod held him. After three more frenzied runs, each shorter than the last and each followed by a leap from the water and violent shaking of the head, the fish was played out. It was a real beauty and easily weighed 7 kg. The sunlight shone on its silver-green body and red fins, and with its vicious razor-sharp teeth it truly looked the king of fish.

Stan stood next to me and as I brought the fish alongside he slid the handle of a gaff under its body, trying to spear the fish. All he managed to do however, was knock the hook right out of its mouth. To this day he claims that it was unintentional, but it did not really matter as soon we were all fishing with small bream as bait and almost immediately hooking into large tiger. For the next hour we enjoyed the most outstanding sport. I found that when we cut off the back fin and tail we were getting even better results. Once we had used up the smaller bream measuring 6 to 8 cm and used larger specimens, the strikes became few and far between.

When we unloaded our catch at the jetty that evening, other anglers who had spent the day on the lake could not believe their eyes as they had all fared very badly. Once again, we had proved that fishing is a scientific sport, and a study of the water and other conditions makes all the difference.

Recipe for Tiger fish

Tiger fish cannot be effectively filleted. The flesh is 'fatty' and the fish should be cut into steaks and grilled in its own fat. A section of the steak will contain small loosely spread interlocking bones. Separate and remove this section and only eat the remainder which will be free of small bones. Prepared and eaten thus, the fish is comparable to grilled barracuda. The fish can also be finely minced and used to make fish cakes.

8 Bass

(Micropterus)

Three types are found in South African waters: large-mouth *(Salmoides)*, small-mouth *(Dolomieu)* and spotted bass *(Punctalatus)*.

Bass are very good table fish. The large and small-mouth bass have similar habits and can be caught with the same angling method. The former is stockier in shape and darker in colour than the latter and the longitudinal marking is more pronounced. It is especially suited to localities where the water is too warm for the small-mouth species which requires clearer and cooler water. Small-mouth bass are basically river fish and their growth in dams is stunted.

The small-mouth bass of the river tends to stay in the same stretch of water, unlike the large-mouth which will swim away with the first flooding of the river. It knows all the refuges and hiding places and when hooked is quick to take advantage of every snag and underwater root in an effort to break the line. As the fish has to fight from birth against the current of the river, it develops a powerful set of fins and tail muscles and is consequently a more powerful fighter than the large-mouth bass. Bass up to 1 kg in weight are easily caught but the larger specimens will test the skill of the most experienced angler. The months of August to October produce the best fishing when the small-mouth spawns. Like the large-mouth, it will usually follow the lure for some distance before striking. When it strikes it seldom takes the lure from behind, but will suddenly streak past the lure and seize it head on or from the side.

Feeding habits

In spring, when the water warms up, the large-mouth bass start to come out of the deeper water into the shallows to feed and spawn. The best time to fish for bass is in the early morning and late afternoon as bass will return to deeper pools of water during the heat of the day. The large bass usually feed well in the evening. They can see a plug in the dark and will take it.

Both species are normally surface feeders. Therefore a surface lure or one which is retrieved just below the surface of the water will usually be more effective than a deep-diving lure. Bass eat insects, baby fish, fledglings, eggs and mice that have fallen into the water, worms, and even small snakes. Thus, a lure resembling any of these may be used. Bass are very temperamental, however, and various lures will have to be tried in accordance with the water conditions.

A much debated question is whether bass strike a lure because of hunger or because they are fighters by instinct and strike to eliminate an enemy or intruder in their waters. I believe that a bass will instinctively strike almost anything in the waters in which it makes its home. I have caught a 0,45 kg bass which on inspection was found to have a huge frog of 170 g inside it. It had

118

obviously eaten its fill when it took my lure. It is clear that during the spawning season bass will fight to protect their large family and will strike a lure as a matter of defence.

Breeding habits

The breeding habits of both species are similar. Bass normally spawn in spring, once the water temperature exceeds 65°F. The male seeks a suitable spawning bed in the shallows and the nest is made in a sheltered spot with a gravelly hard bottom, or amongst fibrous roots. One or more females lay their eggs in the nest which is guarded by the male against invaders. The eggs are kept clean by a gentle fanning movement of the male fish's tail fins. The male does not feed whilst guarding the nest. The eggs hatch in five to ten days. The warmer the water, the quicker the eggs will hatch. Bass spawn when they are two years old and the ovaries taken from a 1 kg large-mouth showed a count of some 79 000 eggs.

Type of rod

A light flexible fast-taper rod, 1,8 to 2,5 m in length, is most suitable to cast the very light lure and play the bass. A rod designed to cast bait with a recessed handle and fitted with a closed-face fixed-spool reel, is perhaps the most effective outfit.

Suitable Spots

Small-mouth bass are often found at the head of a pool or alongside a boulder which breaks the surface of the water, usually forming an eddy. Food accumulates here on its way downstream. It likes deep water and will also be found near hard, sandy or rocky bottoms, in gullies, holes, or the shadowy side of a tree trunk or rock or among tree roots or at the base of rapids. As you get to know the waters you fish, and the habits and haunts of the fish, you will achieve much better and more consistent results. Large-mouth bass like cover and will hide near anything that will shelter them. The more difficult it is to fish in a particular spot, the greater the likelihood of finding a bass there. The big bass are not easily found; they must be looked for in the most awkward spots and tempted with the right lure. A patch of weed or water-lilies or a submerged log are favourite bass haunts. Always watch these spots for a movement that will betray a big bass leaving its hiding place and, without making too much noise or disturbance, try to drop your lure near the movement. An inlet to a dam is always a good spot, as a bass will invariably lie in wait there for food to be washed down. Bass prefer clear water and a spot where the vegetation provides shelter or a spot which has a rocky bottom. Bass are usually also found where a stream runs into a dam, as the oxygen content of fast flowing water is higher than that of stagnant water.

A favourite bass haunt is underneath a dead branch hanging over fairly deep water, on which kingfishers perch and knock their prey. If a plug resembling a minnow is dropped near a bass lying in wait for the bird to drop a fish, it will readily grab it, often the moment the plug hits the water, as the bass will have seen it in the air and made for the spot where it will fall. Bass also have the habit of knocking a lure out of the water and taking it as it falls back into the water. Thus, the angler must start reeling in the plug the moment it alights on the water, remembering to wind in slowly. A slight backward movement with the rod before you start to reel in, imparts life to the lure and also gives the angler an opportunity to take in the slack. If you meet with no success in a particular spot, try the next likely looking spot. Do not be in a hurry to change your lure. There cannot be a fish lying in every spot where you have cast. Give the bass a chance to see your lure. Virtually every type of lure will obtain results if the angler perseveres: valuable time can be lost changing a lure every few minutes if no success is had. The old hands will tell you that the lure which catches the fish is the one in the water. The average angler is doing well with one strike for every 50 to 60 casts. If you catch a bass at a particular spot and find you are not having any more strikes there, try another spot but return to the original spot after a while, as other bass which may have been frightened away may well have returned, as bass have the habit of returning to a particular place.

As many bass dams are filled with weed, it is often necessary to wade. Take great care in wading, however, as the vibration will scare the fish away. They are also able to see you more easily. Do not cast straight out into the deep water; first try casting parallel to the bank close to the weed patches where you are more likely to find a bass lurking. Similarly, if you are able to wade or are fishing from a boat, cast towards the shore and retrieve the lure close to the weed patches.

Bait

None of the natural foods which the bass eats may be used as bait. It should also be noted that it is illegal to use a live fish as bait. Artificial lures resembling insects, tiddlers and other natural foods may be used, however.

Hundreds of different lures are available but most of them are of little value. As you need a selection of lures for different waters and situations, you must build up a suitable collection of reliable lures in the right size and colour, rather than a box full of untested lures. Anglers are a friendly body of sportsmen, always prepared to assist one another, and you will usually find an expert or two at a particular fishing spot who will advise you on the correct type, colour, size and weight of lure to use. The size of the lure is usually determined by the area of the particular stretch of water — the larger the area the larger the lure.

Plugs

Plugs are by far the most popular type of lure used to catch bass. There are many hundreds of different types of lures on the market. Your choice of plugs should be governed by the following factors:

Colour of the water and vegetation

This will affect the colour of the lure you choose. Try to use a lure the colour of which matches that of the surroundings and the type of water life in the dam or river. In muddy water, a yellow lure is the best choice. In clear water, bass will be frightened by a bright and shiny lure. You can dull the colour of your lure by burning it with a match. As most natural bait, such as minnows, to a large extent assume the colour of the water, I prefer to use dark coloured lures

Fishing for bream at Senyati West, Kariba

es Logie in action in the Crocodile River,
Eastern Transvaal

— particularly those with black, dark green or dull gold combinations.

Depth of the water

Use a fast-sinking lure in deep water. By attaching a swivel to the lure or a piece of shot just above the lure, it can be made to dive deeper.

Time of day

The best time to fish for bass is in the early morning or evening. In the evening, a popper retrieved slowly so that it pops along the surface of the water, is irresistible to a bass. In the early morning and late afternoon, a surface plug is usually more successful. During the heat of the day bass move into deeper and cooler water: they are sluggish and a lure must be retrieved very slowly. A lure well suited to these conditions is the rubber worm, tadpole or frog which should be allowed to sink and slowly retrieved along the bottom. I have often found that the larger bass are taken in deeper water and it is not unusual to take a bass in 9 to 12 m of water.

The season

The summer months yield the best fishing for both types of bass. In winter, small-mouth bass are caught more easily than the large mouth. Although large-mouths hibernate and are less active, I have always managed to catch a few, invariably the bigger specimens, by fishing with the right lure in their winter haunts. In winter their metabolism is reduced to the extent that they require only about one-quarter of their usual amount of food. If you look for a gully or crevice in deep water and present an artificial bait that moves and resembles as realistically as possible their natural food, your efforts in braving the cold will most likely be well rewarded. In these conditions I have found the rubber worm fished at a snail's pace along the bottom, to be the most successful lure. I have had the best results with the black and yellow artificial worm followed by the purple worm (although the colour does not match that of any natural food), followed by blue and red worms. The colder the water, the slower should be the rate of retrieval. Conversely, the warmer the water, the faster the rate of retrieval.

Weather conditions

If the water is clear and the sun is shining, choose a darker plug. On a cloudy, darker day, or if the water is dirty, a white plug with a touch of yellow or red is a better choice. When the wind causes the water to become choppy, one will usually find a surface lure less effective, because in these conditions the fish cannot easily discern objects on the surface of the water. Rather use a lure that sinks. The ideal time to catch bass is just before or even during a storm, or after rain or at the tail end of a shower, as the rain beats many little insects down on to the water which are eagerly snapped up by the waiting fish. The bass bug is very effective at such times. When the wind blows, bass tend to linger around reed patches waiting for insects to be dislodged. They will even brush up against reeds in an effort to dislodge them.

Bass will often carefully scrutinise a plug before taking it. Therefore, on some plugs eyes and scale markings are painted

123

with great care. Plastic plugs are often better than wooden plugs, as they are transparent and more fish-like in appearance. It follows, therefore, that you will require a fair selection of lures that contrast in colour, shape and action, and there is much pleasure and fascination in choosing your lures. The satisfaction in catching a bass on a lure is hard to beat. The colour of the lure often makes a tremendous difference to your results. As bass are no more stable in their colour habits than in their feeding habits, it is advisable to have on hand a selection of lures of various colours.

Water temperature

Any stretch of water may be divided into 3 main strata – the surface, the middle strata (the thermocline) and the bottom strata. Bass are usually found in the thermocline where large-mouth bass prefer a temperature of between 20°C and 23°C, and small-mouth bass 18°C to 21°C. Bass do not tend to lie on the bottom of the dam or river.

Spinners

Spinners are also very popular and will often catch a bass which has refused to look at a plug. The spinner causes vibrations in the water which attract bass (and other predatory fish). Many types of spinners are 'weedless' and may be used in spots that are overgrown with weed or water-lilies or some other obstruction, whereas a plug will become snagged in such a spot and you will lose it.

On a bright sunny day, when the water is still and clear, a copper spoon is more successful. On a cloudy day, when the water is rough, a brass or nickel spoon should be used. When you spin in a fast flowing river, the spoon should be weighted to sink deeper, otherwise the current tends to bring it to the surface.

Flies and artificial insects

Special flies have been made for bass fishing. They are larger than trout flies and, unlike trout flies, have a thick soft resilient body.

A fly fisherman often has better results than the bass angler using some other type of lure, but not many anglers are able to cast with trout tackle. The inexperienced angler wishing to try a fly or an artificial insect should use his ordinary equipment and a small bubble float with no weight. This float is transparent and may be partially filled with water to give weight so that the fly may be cast out some distance. A loop in the line should be tied round a piece of match-stick about 0,6 m away from the fly, and a small button fitted on the line between the match and the bubble float to keep the float a set distance from the fly. Unlike a trout, once a bass has a fly in its mouth it won't let it go; so you can strike by lifting the tip of your rod immediately you feel it take your fly. When fishing in a river one should usually cast in the direction the river is flowing and retrieve the lure or fly against the current, as fish swim upstream looking for food.

The action of a lure

The general principle of keeping your bait small applies equally to bass lures. A small lure will usually give the best results, even though a large-mouth bass, as its name implies, has a very large mouth.

Large-mouth Black Bass all caught on trout flies

After the rains, when flying ants come out, bass and all other insect-eating fish will feed readily. A bubble float with no sinker and a trace of 0,6 m may be used to cast an insect type of lure which should bring the best results under these conditions.

The correct action of a lure is very important. Great care must be taken to give the lure the right movement. On some days bass will take any lure offered, even a piece of silver paper wrapped around the hook and pulled through the water. On other days, when the fishing is off, you will not be able to interest the bass in any lure or bait. If the water is clear, the angler will often see a bass disdainfully watching the lure as it is brought past him and even smack it with its tail. If the bass follows the lure but won't take it, tie a trace with a fly attached to it so that it trails some 15 cm behind the lure. This often has the desired result. You can also change the colour of the lure by tying plastic strips of various colours to it. On occasions bass have been known to take only a lure of a certain colour. Alternatively, tie one or two flies of different size on to your line, the larger some 15 cm away from the lure and the smaller the same distance away from that. This gives the impression of the lure (a minnow) chasing the flies and excites the bass which will then take the lure.

Many anglers fish mechanically, casting out and retrieving the lure without thinking how and where it is working. They will catch bass this way, but they will catch far more if they make their lure travel as closely as possible to reed-beds, fallen tree trunks, water-lilies and other likely spots. Moreover, the angler should not retrieve the lure at the same steady pace, but introduce variations of speed and depth by changing the rate of winding and manipulating the tip of the rod.

When fishing with a surface lure, do not always retrieve it immediately. Try to avoid disturbing the water, especially if the surface is calm, as you may well scare away fish. Let the lure lie on the surface for several seconds before starting to retrieve it. Wind in the slack line immediately, however, and keep direct contact with the lure, and be ready to strike if necessary. If nothing happens, jerk the tip of your rod once or twice so that the lure moves a few inches and let it lie still for another few seconds. Then try winding the lure in a foot or two and let it lie still for another few seconds. Repeat this action and try to vary the movement of the lure by pulling gently on the line when the slack has been wound in so that the lure remains in the same spot but shows some signs of life. The more movement you make, the better the action of the lure. Watch your lure carefully. When the bass takes it, you will notice the surface of the water being disturbed. Strike as the lure disappears. It is worth trying to cast your lure on to an object in the water, such as a water-lily, a log or a rock. Impart some movement to the lure by moving the line and after several seconds gently pull it off the object. As it hits the water it may be grabbed by a watchful bass. I have seen a bird alight on a reed which slowly bent over under its weight. The next instant a bass jumped out of the water and grabbed the unsuspecting bird. Often, when a large fish takes your lure it will fight it for several seconds and then the line will suddenly become slack and you will wonder how you lost the fish. The explanation is that the hook probably did not penetrate the bass's powerful jaws, either because the hook was blunt or the fish was holding the lure in its mouth and, after a brief struggle, simply opened its jaws to release the lure. If this happens again try using a small spinner which will be taken deeper into the bass's mouth to lodge the hook properly when you strike. Strike repeatedly to ensure the hook is set.

If the lure dives deep or sinks, allow it to sink to the bottom. You will know it has reached the bottom when your line becomes slack. Start by retrieving it slowly, then jerk the tip of the rod sharply and stop winding for a few seconds. Continue to bring it back by making as many movements as possible at different speeds, but do not retrieve the lure too fast. Repeat this action and your lure will be seized when you least expect it. Small-mouth bass will usually take the lure at the completion of one of the jerking movements. The fact that the large bass are so unpredictable and will bite when least expected makes bass fishing so fascinating. The more slowly the lure is retrieved the better the bass like it.

The rod should be held pointed towards or parallel with the water when you retrieve the lure. If the rod is held at an angle of 45° or upright, the lure will be brought to the surface more quickly.

Fish bait

A dead fish may be used quite successfully as bait. If the fish is small, a long-shanked no. 2 hook should be pushed through the upper half of the bait just below the head. If the dead fish is large, cut it into strips about 8 cm long and thread the hook through the bait so that the tip is at the bottom with plenty of clearance. The top of the bait may be tied to the eye of the hook with a piece of cotton.

Fix a fixed float to your line about 0,6 m above the bait and cast the bait alongside some reeds or water-lilies. Use the smallest possible float that will support your bait. No sinker should be used. Strike the bass immediately the float is pulled under the surface. If you have no results, try pulling your bait slowly past the patch of reeds or water-lilies. You will have more chance of catching a bass this way, as bass will not normally take a dead tiddler.

The bait must have movement and be life-like before it will tempt a bass. This can be achieved by fitting a sinker on to the line just above the hook so that the sinker can be inserted into the tiddler's mouth. When retrieving the bait, wind in for a short distance and then stop. The lead in the fish's mouth causes it to sink head first so that when you start to wind in, the bait wobbles up again, thus giving it a more natural appearance.

Striking

You should not strike the moment you feel the lure being pulled. Rather allow the fish to swim away with it for about 5 to 8 metres, take in the slack, and strike sharply by lifting the tip of the rod some 30 cm. Hold the fish for a few seconds so that the hook sets and then the battle is on. Your drag should be adjusted so that the fish can run if it wishes to. When they are hooked, bass, particularly the big ones, will sometimes jump out of the water and shake their head to and fro in an endeavour to dislodge the lure. Immediately drop the tip of your rod if this happens. A delicate touch is needed speedily to give slack line when the bass jumps out of the water so that you do not take up too much of the line thereby allowing the fish to fall back into the water with a taut line, as the hook is easily loosened and pulled or shaken out of the bass's mouth this way.

Landing a bass

As most lures have three-pronged hooks which easily become entangled in the landing net, I prefer to pick up a bass by hand. This I do by swinging the rod back in an arc, keeping contact with the fish all the time. If you hold the rod in this way, the hook will not be torn out of the fish's mouth nor will the line be broken if the fish should suddenly try to dash off again. Lift the fish's head out of the water and press the thumb of your free hand inside its mouth and grip the underside of its jaw with your forefinger. This grip has a paralysing effect on bass so that you may safely lift it out of the water.

Recipe

Bass, trout and virtually every type of sea or freshwater fish is delicious when cooked in a fish smoker. The fish is simply gutted, carefully dried and left to smoke for 20 to 30 minutes in the smoker. Large fish should first be filleted.

A simple but tasty way of cooking bass, is to stuff it with onion and tomato, season it, and bake it in a mixture of milk and mustard.

At the dam, a bass seasoned and wrapped in tin foil with a pat of butter and thrown into the fire, makes a fantastic lunch.

9 Catfish

(Commonly known as barbel)

There are three types of catfish in South African waters: catfish *(Clarias capensis),* rock barbel *(Grephyoglanis)* and vundu *(Heterobranchus).*

Feeding habits

Catfish will feed on any live or meat bait it finds. It will readily take snails, frogs, grasshoppers, fish both live and dead, birds and soap. Catfish also eat their own spawn as well as any other type of spawn they can find. It will also take rotten meat and animal entrails: the more decayed the meat is, the better the catfish likes it. Do not remove the feathers, when you use a dead bird for bait. Catfish are by no means shy in their feeding habits and if they find a bait, whether large or small, they will immediately take it. Catfish will also take a paste bait. They are great destroyers of other fish.

Breeding habits

Catfish spawn in spring but, unlike other fish, continue to feed whilst they are spawning. The female lays from 30 000 to 50 000 eggs and the fry, which hatch after five or ten days, grow rapidly. Catfish are found in practically all waters as the very hardy spawn survives when it is carried into other waters, usually by certain types of water birds. Their natural enemy is the crocodile.

Suitable spots

An inlet to a dam or river, where food is brought in, is the best spot to choose. Catfish are particularly hardy and will survive when other fish cannot. During a drought when the water dries up they will bury themselves in the mud and remain alive for considerable periods.

Line

A heavier line should be used, as catfish become large and are powerful fighters. A line with a breaking strain of 4,5 kg should be adequate for most waters.

Hook

A fairly large hook should be used, preferably a no. 1 or 2. If you use a large bait, such as a dead bird push two hooks through it, one near the neck and the other at the other end so that the fish will be hooked no matter which part of the bait it takes. The minnow rig described in the chapter on yellow-fish is also very effective in catching catfish.

Sinker

A fairly heavy sinker should also be used to keep the line stationary. A sinker of 40 to 55 gm is a useful weight.

Trace

Two traces may be used. The trace should be made long (25 to 30 cm) so that the bait may be moved around by the current. Ensure that the bait does not lie on the ground but is suspended so that it may dangle. Catfish and yellow-fish watch for any movement and will take a moving bait immediately. The same principle applies when you use a lure of the insect type and a sinker in a river. The trace must be sufficiently long so that it will move freely with the current.

How to strike

There is usually no need to strike a catfish as it will grab the bait and swim with it. When the fish runs with the bait, lift up the rod and by holding the reel keep a little tension on the line for a second or two so that the hook sets in the fish's mouth; then let it run.

A catfish of 9 to 18 kg can be landed on a 5,5 kg line but if there are obstructions in the water the fish may easily be lost. If the fish swims into weeds the only chance you have of landing it is to give it a little slack as the fish may swim out of the weeds and pull the weeds and the line free with it.

Similarly, if when you are playing a fish the line becomes stuck, give a little slack which may enable the fish to free the line as it swims around. In suitable conditions catfish can grow up to 40 kg in weight. A vundu weighing 276,69 kg was taken at Kariba in 1969, although the average size of this species is 18 to 45 kg.

Many large catfish have been caught in the Vaal River. In May 1970, an angler fishing in the Vaal noticed a Black man row out in a corrugated iron canoe to try to land a large fish he had caught. The line had been tied to a tree on the river bank and the water could be seen churning as the fish swam from side to side. The man pulled the fish alongside the canoe. The fish or its weight or both caused the canoe to capsize and the man fell into the river and was drowned. The fish, a catfish, was later pulled in by hand. It weighed 37,66 kg.

The flesh of a catfish is edible and makes very good fish biltong. Because of its appearance it is not a popular table fish, however.

Recipe

Fillet the catfish, season it and simply fry it in deep oil. It makes a tasty and very filling meal.

Klip catfish

This fish rarely exceeds 25 cm in length. It will readily take worms and insects — in fact, any food a fish can eat. Having swallowed the bait it usually swims away and the resultant tug on the line gives the impression that a big fish is biting. As this fish is a bottom-feeder one should use a fixed sinker, a no. 6 hook and a small bait. Take great care in removing the hook as the fish has poisonous spines on its back. A pair of pliers should be used for this.

Silver catfish
Also known as makriel or squeaker

This fish only grows to a weight of between 0,5 and 1 kg but, unlike the other members of the catfish family, is a good table fish. The dorsal fin also has a sharp poisonous spike. A good antidote to the poison is permanganate of potash.

10 Eels

Generally, South African eels are found only in rivers which run east and dams along those rivers into which fresh water flows. Eels can travel considerable distances on land from one stretch of water to another, particularly if the grass is damp so that the surface of their body can remain moist.

Little is known of the migratory habits of eels found in South African waters. Apparently they do not correspond with those of their overseas brethren who make their way to the sea when they are seven to eight years old to spawn and die.

Our eels find their way from rivers into dams where they are often trapped and grow to an immense size. Eels weighing 13 to 18 kg are not uncommon.

By way of an experiment, small eels were caught and ringed below the Victoria Falls. Some years later they were caught in the river above the Falls.

Feeding habits

Eels eat the same type of food as a catfish. They are particularly fond of earthworms, fillets of fish and whole dead fish.

Line

Eels are very powerful fighters and are usually large; therefore, use a line with a breaking strain of 4,5 to 5,5 kg. A firm rod should be used. Once the eel is hooked it should be lifted out of the water promptly before it can wrap its powerful tail around some obstacle. A hard blow on the back of its head will stun it momentarily so that you can quickly wrap some newspaper around it to make it easier to handle.

Hooks

Use a no. 4 to no. 6 hook. Don't use two hooks, for once hooked the eel will make for cover and the second hook may become caught up in some obstruction. Eels are fast swimmers and are rapidly propelled by their powerful tails. They hide in rocky areas or amongst the roots of a submerged tree.

Likely spots

Eels are usually found under trees in which birds nest. If eels are known to be in a particular stretch of water, the following method has often brought results. Fill a large tin with water, add mud and mix until the water is brown. Find an inlet into the dam or river, pour the muddy water into it and fish at that spot. Eels will be attracted by the muddy water which resembles fresh rain water, which usually means food.

How to catch eel

Eels bite very gently and are adept at carefully removing the bait from the hook. For this reason, use a float just large enough to take the weight of a small sinker and the bait. Test the depth of the water and suspend the bait about 30 cm from the bottom. Watch your float carefully. When an eel bites it will move very slowly, normally away from the angler. Strike immediately this happens, unless you are using a dead fish as bait, when you should let the eel run and only strike when it stops. Don't play the eel when it is hooked. Rather drag it straight in as quickly as possible, otherwise the eel will curl around an underwater object and the hook will be torn from its mouth. This applies equally where there is a sudden drop in the river bank or bottom of the dam.

Eel can easily be caught in the following way. Place a mixture of minced liver and bread in a lady's stocking. Insert a stone at the end of the stocking and suspend it from a tree so that it hangs about 45 cm from the bottom of the river or dam. Next morning, slowly lift the stocking out of the water. Eels will suck on the stocking and their teeth will become caught in the mesh.

Once you have landed the eel the battle is by no means over. Like all freshwater fish they are covered with a slippery mucous coating, only much more so than other species of fish. They are impossible to hold as they squirm and twist around vigorously — hence the expression 'slippery as an eel'.

I have watched the comedy of an inexperienced angler trying to place a hooked eel into his keep net. Much to the angler's terror, the eel curled around his arm and eventually escaped back into the water — to the great relief of the angler.

The eel can be incapacitated by being hit on the head with a heavy stick, or pinned down and the vertebrae cut at the point where the head joins the body. Care should be taken not to damage the body, for the bruised or damaged portion becomes inedible. After being skinned and salted, or left to soak in salt water to remove the mucous coat eels should be cut into sections and fried like any other fish. Those who have eaten them regard eels as the finest eating fish and a great delicacy.

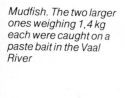

Mudfish. The two larger ones weighing 1,4 kg each were caught on a paste bait in the Vaal River

11 Mud~fish

(Labeo capensis)

Labeo capensis is the most common mud-fish and is usually referred to as the muddie.

Feeding habits

This fish has a heavily-lipped sucking mouth under its head, as well as a sharply rising nape which in larger specimens appears to be almost a deformity. The fish feeds on the river bottom and its natural food consists of moss and other aquatic growth that covers underwater rocks. On occasion, it will also feed on worms and take a paste bait intended for a yellow-fish.

Hook

A very small hook should be used. A no.10 to 12 hook is suitable.

Bait

A good paste bait can be made by mixing flour and water. Stir until the bait has the right consistency – not too hard, too soft, or sticky. A little sugar or custard powder may be added to the mixture. The big muddies will take maize meal flavoured with curry powder. The bait must be kept small – no larger than a pea, so that the fish can easily pick it up. If the bait is too large the muddie will simply suck it.

Float, trace and sinker

The muddie is a very difficult fish to catch. Almost invariably, it will have sucked the bait off the hook by the time the angler tries to strike it. The bite is easily detected, if a small float and hook are used. The shorter the trace, the more easily discernible the bite. If the trace is long enough to allow the bait to lie on the bottom, the fish will suck off the bait without your detecting the bite. Set the float at an angle to the surface and fish close to the bank. The hook should be 6 cm away from the split shot which must be just too heavy for the float (see the 'Lift Method' in the section on Float Fishing). The float will quiver and rise, only to fall full-length on to the surface. After a few seconds the float may be pulled around in a circle. The muddie will suddenly pull your float under but the strike will usually be unsuccessful. Strike when the float lies flat: the fish must have the hook in its mouth for the float to lie flat. Alternatively try a running sinker and a 6 cm trace tied to a swivel. The sinker will keep the line stationary but the trace will move with the current.

The muddie is a very powerful fighter and a fish of 1,5 to 2 kg will test your skill to the full.

Lowveld Muddie
(Labeo rubro-punctatus)

This fish will not take a paste bait but can be caught with a bunch of green moss. The same method and size hook should be used.

Moggel

It does not fight as well as the muddie and does not grow as large. A moggel of 1 kg is a very good catch.

12   Some useful hints

Choosing a suitable spot

Don't fish in the first spot you come to. Look for waterside vegetation and secluded spots where fish seek their food, and those places where food collects, such as the point where currents converge, holes in the river-bed or an inlet or outlet to a dam.

Casting

Your bait will be jerked off the hook if you try to put too much force behind your cast, or if you bring your line to a sudden stop in flight. You will cast further if your spool is fully loaded. Do not overload it, otherwise the line will become 'springy' and slip off the spool.

Bait

When fishing without a sinker in a fast running river, place shot at intervals along your trace, commencing some 30 cm from the bait, to make the bait sink.

   If your paste bait is too soft, add custard or maize meal. If it is too hard, add water and knead well until it has the right consistency.

   The same bait may not be effective two days running. Try various baits until you find the most suitable.

Avoid movement

Do not fish or cast standing up. Do not stand with your back to the sun lest your shadow is cast on the water. Try to find a spot where there is an object behind you. Do not pull your line out of the water every few minutes to examine your bait, unless you have had a few small bites and no action for some time thereafter.

   Remember every movement is a menace to and frightens away fish.

Caught up

If your hook, lure or sinker is caught on the bottom, walk to either side and try pulling it free. If it does not loosen, pull the line until near breaking point and release it suddenly. The rod should be pointing straight to the hook to avoid damaging it. Never pull the rod in an upright position, or it may break. The rod should be held parallel to the water so that when the line is pulled, the strain is on the reel. If you are caught up while playing a fish, give it slack line so that it may swim around and thereby possibly free the line.

Running sinker

To prevent the sinker sliding down to the hook, loop the line around a piece of a match-stick and pull the line tight. You may also whip a piece of coarse nylon on to the line. In this way, you will be fishing with a virtually knot-free line. If a swivel is used, however, there are two extra knots to weaken the line and increase the risk of losing a large fish.

Swivel

A swivel prevents your line from becoming twisted. A snap-on clip permits you to change lures more quickly and efficiently.

Water depth	Cast out a sinker if you wish to test the depth of the water without wading. If the line is taut, the water is shallow; if there is a little slack, it is of medium depth and if there is considerable slack, the water is deep. Two metres is a good average depth for bottom fishing.
Bites	If the fish are biting on the bottom and you are using a fixed sinker and two traces, remove the top trace and tie a swivel on the line next to the sinker and tie the second trace on to the swivel so that both baits may lie on the bottom.
Striking	Never strike on a slack line. If the line becomes slack, it could mean that a fish, having picked up the bait, is swimming towards you. Take in the slack and strike.
Edible fish	Unless the keep net is kept upright the fish may be killed by their own weight and that of the net. They may even go bad if the water temperature is high. The gills will turn yellow and the fish cannot be eaten. If the fish is killed and the gills and entrails removed and the fish kept in a cool place, it will last for several hours.
Lures	Before you start fishing, test your lure at different speeds and depths to ascertain the most effective actions.
Landing net	After each outing wash out the landing net with fresh water to remove the slime and organic matter which would otherwise rot the twine as it decomposes.
Nail-clippers	Use nail-clippers to cut the line, thereby saving a lot of wear and tear on your teeth.
Whetstone	To keep the point of your hook sharp a whetstone should always be in your box.
Lamp	For night fishing use one that has tinted glass which discourages insects. A shield to eliminate eye-strain and excessive light on the water can easily be made from tin foil.
Clothing	Try to wear clothes that blend with the surroundings. Most fish have excellent powers of observation and will spot you long before you see them. Avoid white or brightly coloured clothes. Remember always to wear a hat. The sun in South Africa is harsh and may cause skin cancer.
Earthworms	Cut a 44 gallon drum in half lengthwise and drill some holes in it. Put one section on a trestle the legs of which are stood in tins of water to prevent black ants climbing into the container and eating the earthworms. Fill the container with rich soil which must be kept moist, but not too damp or the worms will drown. A wet sack should be kept over half the container, which must stand in the shade. From time to time, place grass cuttings and old tea-leaves in the container and 2 or 3 times a week sprinkle maize meal lightly on top of the earth.

13   Where to fish

Transvaal

There are many private dams and rivers in the Transvaal which are stocked with fish. The following dams and rivers are the most popular and are for the most part accessible to the general fishing public. For convenience, the towns near which they are situated are listed in alphabetical order:

Amsterdam

The Vaal River has its source at Amsterdam. Yellow-fish and eel are found in the nearby Usutu, Ngwempisi and Umpilusi rivers. Permission to fish (which is rarely refused) must be obtained from the riparian owners. Between Amsterdam and Lothair are several dams which are well stocked with large-mouth black bass and open to the public.

Argent

Good fishing for large-mouth black bass is to be had at the dam near Argent Station.

Barberspan

Barberspan Dam 22 km from Delareyville on the Sannieshof road is well stocked with yellow-fish, carp, mud-fish and catfish.

Barberton

Shiyalongubu Dam (controlled by the Lowveld Fishing Club) has large-mouth black bass and kurper.

Belfast

Belfast Dam is well stocked with bass as are rivers in the district with trout. The permission of the riparian owners must be obtained. The current record trout was caught in nearby Bosbou Dam.

Benoni

Homestead Dam (west of Faramere) has yellow-fish, carp, large-mouth bass, catfish and canary kurper.

Kleinfontein Dam (next to Kleinfontein Mine Dump) has large-mouth black bass, carp, catfish and canary kurper.

Middle Dam (behind Van Riebeeck Hotel), has catfish and carp.

Laundry Dam (in Tom Jones Street, Benoni) also has catfish and carp.

All these dams are controlled by the Rand Piscatorial Association.

Van Dyck Dam (Benoni), controlled by the Van Dyck Club, has yellow-fish, carp and catfish.

Van Dyck Dam (on the Brakpan-Benoni road near the Brakpan Drive-In) is stocked with bass, carp and catfish. The owner charges anglers fifty cents per rod to fish there.

Bospoort Dam (on the Crystal Falls road) is well stocked with small-mouth bass.

Brakpan

Brakpan Dam has carp and catfish. The charge is 10c per rod.

Bronkhorstspruit	Bronkhorstspruit Dam near the fork on the Bronkhorstspruit-Delmas road (take the Waaikraal road) has two sections, Koelkop and Bronkhorstspruit. Better fishing is to be had in the former section and a boat is needed in the latter. Yellow-fish, full-scale and leather carp, catfish and eel are found in the dam.
Carolina	Several dams in the area have been well stocked with large-mouth black bass.
	Yellow-fish, carp and catfish are found in the nearby Komati River and in the new Escom Dam on the Komati River.
Komati River	The Municipal Dam on the Boesmanspruit provides good fishing for yellow-fish. A permit must be obtained from the local angling society.
Delareyville	Barberspan Dam offers good fishing for yellow-fish, carp, mud-fish and catfish.
Dullstroom	The river and dam are stocked with trout. A permit to fish must be obtained from the town clerk. Numerous other streams in the district are stocked with trout. The permission of the riparian owners must be obtained to fish there.
Ermelo	Large-mouth black bass and catfish are found in Pet Dam and Douglas Dam. A dam 6 km from Ermelo on the Sheepmoor road is stocked with large-mouth black bass. A permit obtainable from the Ermelo Angling Society is required to fish in these dams.
Groblersdal	The Olifants River contains kurper and yellow-fish. The permission of the riparian owner must be sought, also that of the Bantu Affairs Commissioner if you wish to fish in a Bantu Trust area.
Haenertsburg	Nearby are the attractive Broederstroom and Helpmekaar rivers which contain trout. (See Magoebaskloof.)
Hartbeespoort Dam	This dam, 40 km west of Pretoria and 72 km north of Johannesburg provides excellent fishing. The dam is fed by the Crocodile and Magalies rivers and several small streams. Kurper up to 2,5 kg, yellow-fish, very large carp of 15 kg and more, gigantic catfish, silverfish, canary kurper and eel are found there. Crocodiles have from time to time been seen in the dam and in 1971 a small crocodile was caught by hand by a boat angler.
Heidelberg	Mud-fish, yellow-fish, carp and catfish are found in the Suikerbos River and Blesbokspruit, both tributaries of the Vaal.
Henley-on-Klip	Between Vereeniging and Johannesburg, provides good fishing for carp and yellow-fish.

Irene   Rietvlei Dam in the Van Riebeeck Nature Reserve is stocked with small-mouth black bass, yellow-fish, carp, kurper and catfish. At one time trout were put into the dam. A permit must be obtained from the Pretoria City Council (or certain sports shops).

Johannesburg area	Emmarentia Dam has carp, bass and catfish. Zoo Lake has carp. These dams are controlled by the Rand Piscatorial Association. Swartkoppies Dam at Jackson's Drift provides fair fishing for bass, trout, yellow-fish, carp and catfish. The dam is controlled by the A.H.V. Club.
Klip River	On the Johannesburg-Vereeniging road: trout, yellow-fish, carp and catfish. This river is not a proclaimed trout stream.
Florida	Florida Lake is stocked with bass, perch, carp and catfish. The lake is controlled by the Rand Leases Angling Club.
Kempton Park	There is good fishing for large-mouth black bass, carp and catfish in Blaupan near the Atlas Ster Drive-in. The charge is 25c per rod.
Klerksdorp	Schoonspruit River provides good fly-fishing for yellow-fish. Carp and catfish are also found in the river. In Klerksdorp Dam there is fair fishing for carp, yellow-fish, mud-fish and catfish.
Lake Chrissie	The lake is stocked with carp and catfish. The permission of the riparian owner is required. Levubu River and Borchers Dam on the river has carp, yellow-fish and catfish. The owner's permission to fish must be obtained.
Loskop Dam	This dam, past Middelburg, offers excellent fishing for kurper, carp, yellow-fish, large-mouth black bass, catfish, makriel (silver catfish) and eel. The dam also contains crocodiles.
Louis Trichardt	Albasini Dam, 28,8 km east of Louis Trichardt on the Levubu River offers yellow-fish, kurper and catfish.
Lydenburg	Lydenburg is the main trout fishing centre of the Transvaal. There are over 50 well stocked streams in the district, one of which is the Dorpspruit which is open the whole year round and the only river where spinning is permitted. Eel are also found in these rivers. The Crocodile River has its source in the area. Tiger fish are found in the lower reaches of this river and at its confluence with the Komati. The permission of the riparian owners must be obtained to fish in most of these streams.
Machadodorp	The Elands River and its tributaries offer trout fishing over an area of some 32 km. These streams are well stocked and as the fishing conditions are easy they are most suitable for beginners.
Magoebaskloof	There is trout fishing to be had in the Helpmekaar and Broederstroom rivers and Stanford Lake. Temporary permits are obtainable from the Lakeside and Magoebaskloof Hotel. A

forestry permit must also be obtained to fish in the Broederstroom. (Spinners may also be used in New Ebenezer Dam which is stocked with trout, bass and kurper). Innumerable private dams in the area are also well stocked with trout and bass.

Marble Hall	Nearby are the Elands and Moss rivers and good kurper fishing is to be had at their junction with the Olifants River. Yellow-fish, carp, very big eel and catfish are also found in the rivers.
Middelburg	The Wilge River which contains kurper, yellow-fish, carp, catfish and eel, runs into Loskop Dam. Several private dams in the area are stocked with large-mouth black bass.
Nyelele Dam	This dam, about 72 km north of Louis Trichardt has kurper, yellow-fish and catfish. Anglers should beware of crocodiles in the dam. A permit is required as the dam is in a Bantu Trust area.
Nylstroom	Excellent kurper fishing is to be had in the Nyl River which rises near Nylstroom.
Pienaars River and Dam	The dam some 33 km north of Pretoria on the Warmbaths-Pretoria road provides very good kurper and large-mouth black bass fishing. Carp, yellow-fish, catfish and eel are also found in the river and dam. The dam is renowned for its very good winter fishing.
Piet Retief	The nearby Pongola, Assegai and Ishlelo rivers contain yellow-fish and catfish.
Potchefstroom	There is good yellow-fish fishing in the nearby Mooi River. Potchefstroom Dam contains yellow-fish, carp, moggel, mud-fish and catfish. Vyfhoek Dam, 8 km from Potchefstroom on the Johannesburg road is well stocked with leather carp.
	Good fishing for large-mouth black bass, yellow-fish, leather and full-scale carp and catfish may be had in Boskop Dam, 20 km west of Potchefstroom.
	Settlers Dam (also known as Klipdrift Dam) is 90 km from Johannesburg on the Potchefstroom road. There is good fishing for yellow-fish, carp, mud-fish and catfish.
Pretoria area	Bon Accord Dam, 14,48 km past Pretoria on the Warmbaths road, offers good fishing for kurper, carp, yellow-fish, catfish and eel.
	Pienaars River and Dam has already been mentioned. Rust de Winter Dam is some 16 km past the Pienaars River Hotel. Carp, yellow-fish, large kurper, mud-fish, the 'bulldog' (a peculiar fish caught on earthworms or fish bait which grows to some 3 kg and is very edible), catfish and eel are found in the dam. Winter fishing is also very good.
Sabie	Trout are to be found in the Sabie River and in the lower reaches yellow-fish, tiger fish and kurper.

Tzaneen	Kurper, yellow-fish and tiger fish are to be found in the Great Letaba River. The riparian owner's permission must be obtained to fish. Merensky Dam is well stocked with kurper and large-mouth black bass.
Vaal River	The Vaal River is the most popular of the Transvaal's many rivers and provides very good angling throughout its reaches. The river rises near Standerton and runs as the border between the Transvaal and the Orange Free State for some 400 km as far as Christiana. Leather and full-scale carp, both the large and small-mouth yellow-fish, silverfish, mud-fish, kurper, catfish, silver catfish and eel are found there. Fishing in the Vaal has deteriorated over the years as a result of industrial development, water pollution and the building of dams which has prevented the annual migration of fish to their spawning beds. For example, angling is prohibited in the immediate area of the barrage as the migrating fish cannot pass the barrage wall and are obliged to deposit their spawn in the shallows where catfish eat most of it.
Vaal Dam	Fish found in the river are also found in the dam.
Ventersdorp	Carp and yellow-fish are found in Rietspruit Dam. A permit is required which is obtainable from the local angling club. There are yellow-fish, carp, mud-fish and catfish in the Schoonspruit River. The permission of the riparian owners must be obtained.
Vereeniging	The confluence of the Vaal, Klip and Suikerbosrand rivers nearby provides good fishing for yellow-fish, carp and catfish. Particularly good fly-fishing is to be had in the rapids. The Klipriver which passes the Lido Hotel on the Johannesburg road has also been stocked with trout and is not a proclaimed trout stream. Henley-On-Klip has been mentioned above. The Visgat River, between Vereeniging and Meyerton, runs into the Vaal River. It contains the same fish as are found in the Vaal.
Volksrust	Two dams in the municipal area are well stocked with large-mouth black bass and bluegill. A permit must be obtained from the Volksrust Angling Club. Yellow-fish and catfish are found in the nearby Sandspruit River which is some 16 km from the town.
Warmbaths	Little Kariba Dam has been stocked with black bass.
Waterberg	The Mogal and Palala Rivers in the area contain yellow-fish, kurper and makriel.
Waterval Boven	Trout are found in the river. A permit must be obtained from the local angling society.

Witbank	There is good fishing for black bass, carp and silverfish in dams in the area.
Wolmaransstad	The dam in the municipal area contains yellow-fish, carp and catfish. Permission to fish must be obtained from the municipality.
Zeerust	This is a good area to fish for yellow-fish, kurper, catfish and eel – in the Groot Marico River, its tributaries and the Elands River. The same types of fish are also found in the dam at Groot Marico.
Natal	Six resorts of the Natal Parks Board provide excellent trout fishing. They are the following:

☐ The Royal Natal National Park is situated 42 km south-west of Bergville. There is trout fishing in the 1 hectare dam below the hotel, containing rainbow, brown and a few brook trout *(Salvelinus fontinalis)*. When weather permits, trout angling is to be had in the Mahai River below the bridge next to the caravan park and in the Tugela. Stocking is done from the hatchery within the park which is well worth a visit. Permits for angling in the dam are obtainable from the Parks Board officer at the hatchery.

Accommodation is provided in the Tendele hutted camp which comprises 13 squaredavels and 2 cottages. There are caravan and camping facilities in the Royal Natal National Park camp, Royal Natal National Park Hotel.

☐ Giant's Castle Game Reserve is 69 km from Estcourt. Fishing is in the Bushman's River for brown trout. Accommodation is provided in a camp with huts, cottages and chalets for 68 guests, with a very comfortable lounge.

☐ Kamberg Nature Reserve is 40 km from Rosetta. The road may be difficult in wet conditions. There is 13 km of brown trout fishing in the Little Mooi River. There are also several small dams holding rainbows and browns. Some excellent brownies have been taken in the dam, but the river fish have generally been very small. The Parks Board recently poisoned that stretch of the river in order to move the greater amount of small fish, and it is hoped that fishing will be of a good standard in two to three years' time. A hatchery has been constructed there.

Accommodation is provided in 5 squaredavels which look down on the picturesque valley. Some 8 km away at Stillerust, a farm-house provides accommodation for 12 people. River fishing is available on the same Little Mooi River.

☐ Himeville Nature Reserve is practically within the boundaries of Himeville. There are two dams holding browns and rainbows. Although fishing has not been of the best over the past few seasons, some specimens of 2 kg of both species have been caught.

Caravanning and camping facilities are available within the park, and excellent accommodation is available at the local hotel or in nearby Underberg.

☐ Coleford Nature Reserve is a very popular resort, 27 km from Underberg, which provides some good rainbow trout fishing in the Ngwangwana River.

There are six squaredavels and five additional rooms. Horses for hire and various amenities such as a tennis court are on hand for the non-angler.

☐ Highmoor Nature Reserve. The angler takes the same route as though to Kamberg Nature Reserve, but continues until the next turn-off to the left. The last five km are steep and the road is poor and not recommended in wet weather. There are two dams which contain rainbows and browns and in which experiments have been carried out with brook trout and tiger trout (a cross between brook and brown trout). The dams have a good reputation for fishing which, in my opinion, is well deserved. Brown trout are not too frequently taken, but specimens of up to 3,5 kg have been caught, while rainbows of two kg are common. Cars must be left at the Forestry buildings and anglers must walk 2,5 km to the dams. A camping area is also sited. A permit is required which can be obtained at the Forestry offices.

There are two major trout angling clubs in Natal which also provide excellent fishing and facilities.

☐ Natal Fly Fisher's Club (NFFC). The NFFC was formed early in 1972 under the chairmanship of John Beams. Its growth over the past five years has been rapid, and it now controls beats on the Mooi River, Lion's River, Elands River, Amanzinyama River, the Little Mooi, Hlatikulu River, Umgeni River and the Yarrow River. It also controls fishing in nine trout dams. The Club has not only concentrated on trout; there are also three black bass dams. Both rainbows and browns are stocked in the dams and fish of 1 kg or more are common.

☐ Underberg – Himeville Trout Angling Club. This club was formed in 1954 and is one of the foremost angling clubs in Natal. Unlike so many trout angling clubs whose headquarters are some distance from their waters, the Underberg-Himeville Club is controlled from its rondavel at the Underberg Hotel not far from the sparkling waters of the Umzimkulu. Over 160 km of rainbow trout fishing is to be had on the Umzimkulu, Polela and Ngwangwana, and a few kilometres of brown trout fishing in the Umkomazana and Loteni. The club also controls ten still waters in which excellent fly fishing may be experienced, there are some monster fish, such as the 4,38 kg rainbow that Billy Hughes' dam yielded. Other worthwhile dams to fish are McDougall's dam and Turner's dam.

Private fishing

In addition to the Parks Board waters and those controlled by the trout fishing clubs, there are acres upon acres of prime waters on private land. Dams boasting an average catch of over 1,5 kg are not too uncommon: even fish of 2,5 kg create little interest. Examples of these are the 4,66 kg rainbow taken by Frank Stacey, a rainbow of 5,04 kg taken in Le Sueurs dam in October 1976 and a 4,78 kg cock fish captured by C.S. Barlow in his dam at Balgowan. Aspirant anglers wishing to fish in these waters, will naturally have to show the necessary respect for another's property. Too often, though, only a personal introduction from the owner will suffice.

Most of the Natal rivers flowing through areas unsuitable for trout hold a variety of fish that will afford the angler good sport. These include the scaly (also called the Natal yellow-fish *(Barbus Natalensis)* which does not grow to great proportions. A fish of 1,5 kg is a good capture, but the fish is recognised as a worth-while foe. It is not averse to taking an artificial fly in clear water. Although paste baits have been concocted, natural baits such as crickets, earthworms, frogs and crabs are very successful. Of course such titbits are also to the liking of the ubiquitous catfish. Eels are generally taken by night anglers prepared for the tug of war that will ensue.

Tiger-fish are not widespread but are encountered in Northern Natal and Zululand.

Generally, all these fish except tiger-fish are found in Natal rivers, such as the Incandu (Newcastle), the Buffalo (Utrecht), Klip and Tugela (Ladysmith), Umgeni (Howick), Black Umfolozi, White Umfolozi and the Pongola near Gollel.

While many anglers prefer the quiet of the river bank, there is no doubt that next to trout, the black bass is enthusiastically sought after. Small-mouthed black bass are found in running waters such as the Umgeni near Howick and the Bushman's and the Mooi.

Natal has many still waters which in addition to the fish already mentioned, provide sanctuary for the popular large-mouthed black bass *(Micropterus salmoides)*.

Forage fish, excepting the small indigenous barbus, are the red-breasted tilapia *(Melanopleura),* vlei kurper *(Tilapia sparrmanii)* the redfin 'Tilapia' and the imported bluegill sunfish *(Lepomis macrochirus).*

The blue gill is a good fighting fish for its size and will take spinner and fly, but one is often hard put to find any of decent proportions.

Midmar Dam (Lake Midmar) is an angler's paradise, it is nearby the Natal Parks Board and is shared with other water sports such as yachting and speed-boating. Accommodation is offered in chalets, and a number of caravan and camping sites are available. There is a restaurant near the main complex.

Some years ago bass anglers had first-class sport with spotted bass and large-mouth bass, but recently bank angling seems to have declined, although many lunkers still abound.

I do believe that some day a South African record carp will be taken here. One has only to survey the water surface at first light to see the number of huge carp rolling around!

Also close to Pietermaritzburg are Henley Dam and Peatties Lake. Nagle Dam, an imposing water, also has the usual complement of fish, while at Greytown is Merthley Lake in which the South African record brown trout (4,53 kg) was taken in 1935 Twenty years ago a few rainbows of up to 4 kg also fell to angler' wiles. The lake was drained some years ago, however, but by all accounts efforts are now being made to re-establish the bass fishing.

Other worth-while bass dams are the Pumula Dam (Ladysmith and Tom Worthington Dam near Dundee.

Countless small empoundments considered unsuitable for

trout, are stocked with bass by their owners. There are many of these private enclosures, especially in the Mooi River and Nottingham Road areas.

Cape

The following waters are stocked with trout:

Wemmerhoek Reservoir – rainbow trout

Wemmer River – rainbow trout

Steenbras Reservoir – rainbow, brown and tiger trout

Vogelvlei – large and small-mouth bass

Paarl Mountain Reservoirs – Bethal and Nantes Dams are stocked with rainbow trout

Stellenbosch Municipal Reservoir – rainbow trout

Rietvlei Dam, Koubokkeveld – rainbow trout

Buffelsrivier Dam, Pringle Bay – rainbow, brown and tiger trout

Upper Breede River – rainbow trout

Ceres Arch Dam – rainbow trout

Liesbeek River – rainbow trout

Orange Kloof Stream, Hout Bay – rainbow trout

Smalbaar River and tributaries, Du Toit's Kloof – rainbow trout

Molenaars Fishery, Du Toit's Kloof – rainbow trout

Holmsloot River – rainbow trout

Witte River, Bainskloof – brown and rainbow trout

Eerste River – rainbow trout

Dwars River, Banhoekkloof – rainbow and brown trout

Twenty-Four Rivers, Salem – rainbow trout, small-mouth bass and kurper

Witels River, Michael's Pass, Ceres – brown trout

Jan Dut Toit's River – rainbow trout.

Orange Free State

There are several large dams in the Orange Free State, which are available to the public for fishing. These include the following: Vaal Dam – (Vaal River), Allemanskraal Dam (Sand River), Erfenis Dam – (Vet River), Bloemhof Dam – (Vaal River), Rustfontein Dam – (Modder River), Krugersdrift Dam – (Modder River), Kalkfontein Dam – (Riet River) and Tierpoort Dam – (Kaffir River).

The most common species in these dams are: small-mouth yellow-fish, mud-fish, barbel, carp and the Orange River mud-fish.

The large-mouth yellow-fish is found in Vaal Dam and Kalkfontein Dam. The preferred angling species in these dams are small-mouth yellow-fish, barbel and carp.

Small and large-mouth black bass, are found mainly in farm dams in the eastern and north-eastern parts of the Orange Free State. The five most common fish species occur in all river systems in the province.

Twenty-fifth record fish log for the year ending 31 December 1976

W. J. van den Berg
Freshwater Record Officer

Key to Districts

WP	Western Province Angler's Union	T	Transvaal Angler's Union
EP	Eastern Province Angler's Union	ST	Southern Tvl. Angling & Casting Union
EL	East London & Border Angler's Union	NT	Northern Tvl. Angling & Casting Union
N	Natal Angling Board of Control	ET	Eastern Tvl. Angling & Casting Union
GW	Griqualand West Angler's Union	SWA	South-West Africa Angler's Union
O	OFS Angler's Union	SW	Swaziland Angler's Club
WT	West. Tvl. Angling Board of Control		

Light tackle class

Common Name	Scientific Name	Weight	Place	Angler	District	Line	Year
Catfish	Clarias gariepinus	17,984 kg	Vaal River	Booysen, C.P.	ST	,21	1975
Rock Barbel	Gephyroglanis sclateri	0,567 kg	Vaal River	Pretorius, J.	WT	,20	1968
Carp (Mirror)	Cyprinus Carpio	21,850 kg	Hartbeespoort Dam	Barrow, L.E.	ST	,22	1959
Carp (Common)	Cyprinus carpio	12,850 kg	Vaal River	Pretorius, J.S.	WT	,22	1971
Black Bass (LM)	Micropterus salmoides	3,095 kg	Private dam	Levin, I.H.	ET	,21	1969
Black Bass (SM)	Micropterus dolomieu	1,987 kg	Loskop Dam	Stander, G.S.	T	,22	1965
Spotted Bass	Micropterus punctulatus	0,940 kg	Midmar Dam	Veldman, H.C.	N	,21	1972
Bluegill	Lepomis macrochirus	0,993 kg	D.N.C. Dam	Poole, G.F.	N	,20	1968
Madagascar Mottled Eel	Anguilla marmorata	4,570 kg	Spioenkop Dam	Cerronio, P.C.	N	,20	1976
Eel (Common)	Anguilla mossambica	4,117 kg	Limpopo River	Nicosia, G.G.	T	,21	1960
Kurper (Vlei)	Tilapia sparmanii	0,312 kg	Bronkhorstfontein	Visser, A.F.	T	,15	1973
Kurper (Canary)	Chetia flaventris	0,375 kg	Pienaarsriver Dam	Schoeman, M.P.	T	,18	1972
Kurper (Blue)	Tilapia mossambica	2,980 kg	Loskop Dam	Bezuidenhout, C.J.W.	NT	,21	1973
Kurper (Israel)	Tilapia area	1,860 kg	Farm Dam CP	Rose-Innes, H.	WP	,21	1971
Kurper (Redbreast)	Tilapia melanopleura	1,845 kg	Loskop Dam	Gerber, H.J.	ST	,20	1960
European Perch	Perca fluviatilis	1,100 kg	Florida Lake	Smit, J.	ST	,17	1975
Yellow-fish (SM)	Barbus holubi	5,521 kg	Vaal River	Vermeulen, J.G.	WT	,22	1970
Yellow-fish (LM)	Barbus kimberleyensis	10,508 kg	Vaal River	Grobler, P.	T	,20	1951

Common Name	Scientific Name	Weight	Place	Angler	District	Line	Year
Scaly	*Barbus natalensis*	3,380 kg	Umgeni River	Little, R.G.	N	,20	1974
Yellow-fish (SS)	*Barbus polylepis*	2,299 kg	Pongola River	Kotze, P.D.	N	,22	1970
Silverfish	*Barbus mattozi*	1,355 kg	Hartbeespoort Dam	Gerber, B.	ST	,20	1961
Sawfin	*Barbus serra*	0,860 kg	Doorn River CP	Vilonel, C.G.	NT	,20	1973
Shovelmouth	*Varicorhinus nelspruitensis*	0,865 kg	Bloemveld Dam	Engelbrecht, G.E.	N	,23	1974
Sawfin	*Barbus serra*	1,580 kg	Doorn River CP	Vilonel, C.G.	NT	,20	1973
Clanwilliam Yellow-fish	*Barbus capensis*	1,887 kg	Doorn River CP	Vilonel, C.G.	NT	,21	1964
Trout (Brown)	*Salmo trutta*	2,555 kg	Municipal Dam	Botha, M.L.	O	,23	1954
Tiger Trout	*Trutta X salvelinus*	1,420 kg	Steenbras Dam	Beales, P.E.	WP	,21	1976
Trout (Rainbow)	*Salmo gairdneri*	3,875 kg	Golden Gate OFS	Nel, A.	O	,20	1971
Tench	*Tinca tinca*	1,410 kg	Breede River	Cousin, George	WP	,22	1975
		1,600 kg	Breede River	Lochner, J.O.	WP	,21	1976
		1,710 kg	Breede River	Taylor, M.A.	WP	,20	1976
		1,980 kg	Breede River	Lochner, J.	WP	,21	1976
Red-lip	*Labeo rosea*	2,157 kg	Elands River Tvl	Borman, P.A.	T	,18	1958
Mud-fish	*Labeo umbratus*	1,820 kg	Vaal River	Muller, D.J.	WT	,19	1973
Clanwilliam Sandfish	*Labeo sceberi*	0,284 kg	Olifants River	Du Plessis, J.	WP	,20	1966
Mud-fish	*Labeo capensis*	2,448 kg	Vaal River	Cumming, G.A.	ST	,23	1967
Red-scale Mud-fish	*Labeo rubropunctatus*	1,080 kg	Crocodile River	Labuschagne, B.W.J.	ET	,20	1976
Spot-tail	*Alestes imberi*	0,300 kg	Crocodile River	Labuschagne, B.W.	ET	,16	1971
Mud-fish (Tugela)	*Labeo rubromaculatus*	1,200 kg	Chelmsford Dam	Crossman, S.G.	N	,21	1974

Medium tackle class

Common Name	Scientific Name	Weight	Place	Angler	District	Line	Year
Bluegill	*Lepomis macrochirus*	1,055 kg	Durnacol Dam 11	Katzke, J.R.	N	,26	1973
Catfish	*Clarias gariepinus*	24,535 kg	Vaal River	Herwig, H.W.	T	,29	1964
Carp (Mirror)	*Cyprinus carpio*	18,770 kg	Hartbeespoort Dam	Botha, Mrs. A.C.	T	,30	1959
Carp (Common)	*Cyprinus carpio*	16,924 kg	Vaal River	Nel, G.S.	ET	,30	1971

Common Name	Scientific Name	Weight	Place	Angler	District	Line	Year
Silverfish	*Barbus mattozi*	1,260 kg	Hartbeespoort Dam	Van Staden, W.	T	,24	1952
Trout (Rainbow)	*Salmo gairdneri*	3,123 kg	Linsklip River	Cullinan, D.M.	NT	,29	1967
Makreel	*Eutropius depressirostris*	1,050 kg	Komati River	Van der Westhuizen, J.	ET	,30	1975
Trout (Brook)	*Salvelinus fontinalis*	1,035 kg	Grootgewacht Dam	Neale, R.S.	N	,30	1975
Mud-fish	*Labeo capensis*	2,967 kg	Standerton Dam	Schoeman, J.J.	ET	,30	1971
Lead-fish	*Labeo molybdinus*	1,533 kg	Hartbeespoort Dam	Botha, J.J.J.	T	,24	1961
Mud-fish	*Labeo rubropunctatus*	3,407 kg	Limpopo River	Van Niekerk, G.R.	N	,28	1962
Mud-fish (Tugela)	*Labeo rubromaculatus*	1,610 kg	Buffalo River	Homan, N.	N	,26	1976
European Perch	*Perca fluviatilis*	1,305 kg	Roodepoort Dam	Healey, Mrs. D.	T	,24	1961
Black Bass (LM)	*Micropterus salmoides*	4,200 kg	Rietvlei Dam	Oelofse, J.A.	NT	,31	1973
Black Bass (SM)	*Micropterus dolomieu*	2,495 kg	Private Dam	Smuts, T.F.	N	,32	1972
Spotted Bass	*Micropterus punctulatus*	2,040 kg	Midmar Dam	Willers, E.D.	N	,31	1973
Bottle-nose	*Mormyrus longirostris*	6,730 kg	Zambezi River	Struyveldt, W.F.	WT	,26	1969
Tiger-fish	*Hydrocynus vittatus*	6,361 kg	Zambezi River	Cummings, D.	ST	,31	1962
Chessa	*Distichodus schenga*	3,861 kg	Deka, Zambezi River	Du P. Venter, A.	T	,32	1971
Mud-fish	*Labeo umbratus*	2,853 kg	Van Dyks Dam	Inggs, D.	T	,29	1962
Flat-head Mullet	*Mugil cephalus*	2,640 kg	Mt. Edgecombe Dam	Kidd, P.	N	,32	1969
Tench	*Tinca tinca*	0,587 kg	Breede River CP	Pieters, W.J.	WP	,30	1969
Bulldog	*Gnathonemus macrolepidotus*	0,319 kg	Rust-der-Winter Dam	Badenhorst, J.	T	,31	1961
Rock Barbel	*Gephyroglanis sclateri*	0,546 kg	Vaal River	Bell, F.J.	T	,24	1962
Squeaker	*Syndontis Zambezensis*	0,290 kg	Crocodile River	Herbst, J.L.	ET	,31	1976
Eel(Common)	*Anguilla mossambica*	4,400 kg	Witbank Dam	Grundling, J.C.	ET	,26	1976
Eel (African Mottled)	*Anguilla nebulosa labiata*	8,405 kg	Umfolozi River	De Villiers, W.M.	SW	,28	1954
Kurper (Israel)	*Tilapia aurea*	1,476 kg	Farm Dam CP	Slaughter, S.G.	WP	,25	1970
Kurper (Canary)	*Chetia flaviventris*	0,440 kg	Letaba Catchment	Dekenah, A.V.	T	,24	1961
Kurper (Blue)	*Tilapia mossambica*	3,030 kg	Loskop Dam	Van Rensburg, D.J.J.	ST	,30	1976
		3,265 kg	Loskop Dam	Storm, A.	NT	,29	1976

Common Name	Scientific Name	Weight	Place	Angler	District	Line	Year
Yellow-fish (SM)	*Barbus holubi*	6,758 kg	Vaal River	Van der Westhuizen, G.	ST	,25	1959
Yellow-fish (LM)	*Barbus kimberleyensis*	13,800 kg	Vaal River	Coetzee, G.	T	,26	1960
Yellow-fish (LS)	*Barbus marequensis*	5,115 kg	Crocodile River	Van Sittert, F.P.J.	ET	,24	1972
Scaly	*Barbus natalensis*	4,628 kg	Mooi River N	Bridge, W.D.	N	,24	1956
Clanwilliam Yellow-fish	*Barbus capensis*	5,679 kg	Olifants River CP	Pieters, W.J.	WP	,30	1969
Red-lip	*Labeo rosea*	2,060 kg	Rust-der-Winter Dam	Swart, M.J.	NT	,31	1973
Yellow-fish (SS)	*Barbus polylepis*	5,760 kg	Crocodile River	Nel, F.C.	ET	,37	1974
Sawfin	*Barbus serra*	3,040 kg	Olifants River CP	Walters, M.H.L.P.	WP	,28	1973
Tench	*Tinca tinca*	3,861 kg	Paardevlei CP	Pieters, W.J.	WP	,24	1970
Cape Whitefish	*Barbus andrewi*	2,610 kg	Breede River CP	Schneider, N.	WP	,31	1973
Vlei Kurper	*Tilapia sparrmanii*	0,305 kg	Private Dam	Van der Merwe, A.	NT	,31	1971

All tackle class

Common Name	Scientific Name	Weight	Place	Angler	District	Line	Year
Barbel	*Clarias gariepinus*	31,805 kg	Vaal River	Rabie, F.J.	GW	,48	1968
Vundu	*Heterobranchus longifilis*	27,079 kg	Lake Kariba	Barnard, J.S.	WT	,41	1968
Black Bass (SM)	*Micropteris dolomieu*	1,717 kg	Rietvlei Dam	Stegman, N.D.	T		1965
Black Bass (LM)	*Micropterus salmoides*	3,920 kg	Private Dam	Taljaard, J.J.J.	ET	,40	1976
Blue Gill	*Lapomis machrochirus*	0,880 kg	Saunders Dam	Girdwood, R.I.	SW		1952
Bulldog	*Gnathonemus macrolepidotus*	0,333 kg	Rust-der-Winter Dam	Starck, K.H.	T		1960
Carp (Mirror)	*Cyprinus carpio*	24,421 kg	Mazoe Dam (Rhodesia)	Hill, B.	N		1965
Carp (Common)	*Cyprinus carpio*	16,981 kg	Vaal River	Steyn, P.H.	ST		1962
Eel (African Mottled)	*Anguilla nebulosa labiata*	20,638 kg	Crocodile River	Mare, P.I.	ET	,50	1971
Eel (Common)	*Angilla mossambica*	5,452 kg	Kariba Zambezi	Van Zyl, J.C.	WT	,33	1967
Eel (Madagascar)	*Anguilla marmorata*	14,448 kg	Tugela River	Dicks, F.	N		1971
Kurper (Redbreast)	*Tilapia melanopleura*	1,398 kg	Loskop Dam	Barnard, C.P.	T		1954
Kurper (Blue)	*Tilapia mossambica*	2,850 kg	Loskop Dam	Harding, R.P.	ST	,36	1974
Kurper (Vlei)	*Tilapia Sparrmanii*	0,302 kg	Bronkhorstfontein	Van Deventer, W.A.	T	,33	1971

Common Name	Scientific Name	Weight	Place	Angler	District	Line	Year
Tench	*Tinca tinca*	1,006 kg	Breede River	Cousin, George	WP	,37	1976
Whitefish	*Barbus andrewi*	3,407 kg	Hospital Dam	Buitendag, J.	WP	,39	1969
Sawfin	*Barbus serra*	2,200 kg	Olifants River CP	Alers, D.D.C.	WP	,37	1974
Silverfish	*Barbus mattozi*	0,624 kg	Rust-der-Winter Dam	Steenkamp, C.E.	NT	,33	1968
Bream (Kariba)	*Tilapia mortimeri*	2,498 kg	Kariba Zambezi	Gerber, H.J.	WT	,33	1967
Kurper (Canary)	*Chetia flaviventris*	0,383 kg	Hartebeespoort Dam	De Klerk, J.L.	T		1959
Makreel	*Eutropius depressirostris*	0,915 kg	Groblersdal	De Jager, C.	T		1957
Mud-Fish	*Labeo capensis*	2,839 kg	Vaal River	Cockeran, Mrs. J.F.	O		1965
Mud-Fish	*Labeo umbratus*	1,873 kg	Taaibosspruit	De Kock, P.J.	O		1954
Red-Lip	*Labeo rosea*	1,803 kg	Letaba River	Thomson, E.J.	T		1963
Rock Barbel	*Gephyroglanis Sclateri*	0,454 kg	Vaal River	Kruger, G.P.W.	GW		1965
Squeaker	*Synodontis zambezensis*	0,227 kg	Loskop Dam	Van Rensburg, S.J.	WT	,40	1971
Trout (Rainbow)	*Salmo gairdneri*	2,668 kg	Otto Dam	Schepp, J.J.	T		1956
Tiger-Fish	*Hydrocynus vittatus*	12,693 kg	Zambezi River	Cumming, G.A.	ST		1962
Clanwilliam	*Barbus capensis*	1,710 kg	Doorn River CP	Vilonel, C.G.	NT	,45	1973
Yellow-Fish (LM)	*Barbus kimberleyensis*	21,400 kg	Vaal Dam	Barnard, M.C.	T	,37	1972
Yellow-Fish (SM)	*Barbus holubi*	7,837 kg	Kraaipoort Dam	Oberholzer, J.J.	O		1957
Yellow-Fish (SS)	*Barbus polylepis*	6,180 kg	Crocodile River	Potgieter, J.T.	ET	,46	1975
Cornish Jack	*Mormyrops deliciosus*	7,724 kg	Kariba Zambezi	Gerber, H.J.	WT	,33	1967
Chessa	*Distichodus schenga*	4,472 kg	Zambezi River	Jooste, F.J.	NT	,36	1973

Junior Section

The number in brackets following the youngster's name indicates his age.

Light tackle class

Barber	*Clarias gariepinus*	9,900 kg	Grootvlei Dam	Koekemoer, J.M.	T	,20	1970
Carp (Mirror)	*Cyprinus carpio*	10,364 kg	Hartbeespoort Dam	Stander, P. (7)	WT	,20	1970

Common Name	Scientific Name	Weight	Place	Angler	District	Line	Year
Carp (Common)	*Cyprinus carpio*	10,023 kg	Hartbeespoort Dam	Stander, K. (9)	WT	,28	1970
Tench	*Tinca tinca*	0,410 kg	Breede River CP	Schneider, R. (16)	WP	,22	1972
Blue Gill	*Lepomis machrochirus*	1,100 kg	P.D. Ladysmith	Greyling, M. (12)	N	,20	1975
Yellow-Fish (SS)	*Barbus polylepis*	2,020 kg	Rondebosch	Spencer, A. (11)	ET	,19	1975
Scaly	*Barbus natalensis*	1,675 kg	Chelmsford Dam	Lötter, L.J. (11)	N	,19	1975
Kurper (Canary)	*Chetia flaviventris*	0,212 kg	Hartbeespoort Dam	Stander, K. (9)	WT	,20	1970
Kurper (Blue)	*Tilapia mossambica*	1,275 kg	Roodeplaat Dam	Botha, W.J. (15)	NT	,20	1975
Kurper (Vlei)	*Tilapia sparmanii*	0,270 kg	Private Dam	Makins, S.R. (10)	N	,21	1972
Eel (Common)	*Anguilla mossambica*	0,840 kg	Buffalo River	Vermaak, J.S. (15)	N	,15	1972
Mud Mullet	*Labeo umbratus*	0,820 kg	Rondebosch Dam	Van der Merwe, J. (15)	ET	,19	1976
Tugela Mud-Fish	*Labeo rubromaculatus*	0,730 kg	Chelmsford Dam	Greyling, M. (10)	N	,20	1974
Mud-Fish	*Labeo capensis*	1,959 kg	Boskop Dam	Thomson, K. (11)	ST	,22	1965
Red-Scaled Mud-Fish	*Labeo rubropunctatus*	1,180 kg	Crocodile River	Labuschagne, H. (12)	ET	,20	1976
Black Bass (LM)	*Micropterus salmoides*	2,460 kg	Private Dam	Blom, P.A. (13)	WP	,20	1976
Black Bass (SM)	*Micropterus dolomieu*	1,105 kg	Breede River CP	Schneider, R. (16)	WP	,22	1972
Rock Barbel	*Gephyroglanis sclateri*	0,326 kg	Wilge River	Van Rensburg, J. (18)	O	,22	1969
Squeaker	*Syndotus zambezensis*	0,090 kg	Pongola River	Van der Westhuizen, B.C.	N	,23	1972
Trout (Rainbow)	*Salmo gairdneri*	2,782 kg	Belfast Privat Dam	Campher, T. (12)	ST	,20	1971
Minnow (Three Spot)	*Barbus trimaculatus*	0,070 kg	Hartbeespoort Dam	Van Rensburg (11)	WT	,22	1971

Medium tackle class

Minnow (Three Spot)	*Barbus trimaculatus*	0,021 kg	Marico River	Le Roux, H.J. (14)	T	,32	1968
Catfish	*Claria gariepinus*	17,720 kg	Vaal Dam	Van der Merwe, P. (12)	T	,30	1970
Yellow-Fish (SM)	*Barbus holubi*	4,145 kg	Vaal River	Nebe, W. (14)	WT	,30	1968
Blue Gill (Sunfish)	*Lepomis macrochirus*	0,790 kg	Private Dam, Worcester	Schneider, R.A. (16)	WP	,31	1972
Black Bass (SM)	*Micropterus dolomieu*	1,348 kg	Olifants River CP	Botha, M.D.	WP	,30	1967

Common Name	Scientific Name	Weight	Place	Angler	District	Line	Year
Black Bass (LM)	*Micropterus salmoides*	2,480 kg	Private Dam	Blom, P.A. (13)	WP	,32	1976
Spotted Bass	*Micropterus punctulatus*	1,842 kg	Midmar Dam	Fourie, Shane (13)	N	,30	1972
Kurper (Blue)	*Tilapia mossambica*	2,726 kg	Loskop Dam	Dippenaar, J. (14)	NT	,30	1972
Carp (Common)	*Cyprinus carpio*	15,550 kg	Vaal River	Visser, Miss M.C. (10)	WT	,31	1974
Carp (Mirror)	*Cyprinus carpio*	12,409 kg	Wilge River	Joubert, I.J. (11)	O	,32	1968
Tench.	*Tinca tinca*	0,780 kg	Breede River CP	Schneider, R. (16)	WP	,31	1972
Yellow-Fish (LM)	*Barbus kimberleyensis*	10,320 kg	Vaal Dam	Van Wyk, R. (13)	T	,31	1973
Silverfish	*Barbus mattozi*	0,581 kg	Rust-der-Winter Dam	Van der Merwe, J.P. (14)	NT	,32	1967
Gorge-Fish	*Barbus codringtoni*	4,260 kg	Zambezi River	Botha, W.J. (13)	N	,26	1973
Sawfish	*Barbus serra*	2,235 kg	Olifants River CP	Botha, M. (8)	WP	,30	1967
Whitefish	*Barbus andrewi*	2,384 kg	Breede River CP	Schneider, R. (15)	WP	,30	1971
Yellow-Fish (SS)	*Barbus polylepis*	5,200 kg	Crocodile River	Nel, David (11)	ET	,31	1974
Scaly	*Barbus natalensis*	2,383 kg	Ingagane River	Davel, L. (11)	N	,27	1970
Kurper (Canary)	*Chetia flaviventris*	0,105 kg	Hartebeespoort Dam	Louw, A.K. (8)	T	,27	1972
Mud-Fish (Rednose)	*Labeo rosea*	1,431 kg	Rust-der-Winter Dam	De Wet, G. (10)	NT	,30	1972
Kurper (Vlei)	*Tilapia sparmenii*	0,280 kg	Durbanville CP	King, M.E. (15)	WP	,31	1975
Mud-Fish	*Labeo capensis*	2,654 kg	Vaal River	Griesel, J. (14)	O	,24	1970
Clanwilliam	*Labeo seeberi*	0,269 kg	Olifants River	Du Plessis, J. (19)	WP	,26	1966
Mud Mullet	*Labeo umbratus*	0,929 kg	Vaal River	Walker, R.D. (14)	T	,28	1968
Eel (Madagascar)	*Anguilla marmorata*	3,600 kg	Privana River	Van Niekerk, Kobus (15)	N	,25	1974
Eel (Common)	*Anguilla mossambica*	1,105 kg	Breede River CP	Schneider, R. (16)	WP	,31	1972
Barbel	*Clarias gariepinus*	21,922 kg	Vaal River	Maritz, F. (15)	WT	,41	1968
Blue Gill	*Lepomis machrochirus*	0,241 kg	Private Dam CP	Wyness, G. (7)	WP	,47	1967
Black Bass (LM)	*Micropterus salmoides*	2,384 kg	Midmar Dam	Barthorpe, G.J. (11)	N	,35	1971
Spotted Bass	*Micropterus punctulatus*	1,050 kg	Midmar Dam	Barthorpe, G.J. (11)	N	,36	1971
Black Bass (SM)	*Micropterus dolomieu*	1,703 kg	Olifants River	Van der Westhuizen, B. (14)	WP	,33	1967
Carp (Mirror)	*Cyprinus carpio*	15,491 kg	Buffelspoort Dam	Smit, B.S. (14)	NT	,38	1972

Common Name	Scientific Name	Weight	Place	Angler	District	Line	Year
Carp (Common)	Cyprinus carpio	13,133 kg	Hartebeespoort Dam	Oosthuizen, A. (14)	NT	,37	1969
Tiger-Fish	Hydrocynus vittatus	9,995 kg	Kariba, Zambezi	Stander, M. (9)	NT	,55	1963
Silverfish	Barbus mattozi	0,805 kg	Roodeplaat Dam	Van Niekerk, L.J. (15)	NT		1975
Tench	Tinca tinca	1,378 kg	Breede River CP	Schneesberger, K. (16)	WP		1975
Makreel	Eutropius depressirostris	0,354 kg	Cramers Dam	Sonnenberg, S. (14)	NT	,33	1967
Yellow-Fish (LM)	Barbus kimberleyensis	15,350	Vaal Dam	Van Wyk, B. (14)	T	,39	1973
Yellow-Fish (SM)	Barbus holubi	4,770 kg	Vaal River	Theron, P. (13)	O	,43	1968
Yellow-Fish (SS)	Barbus polylepis	4,543 kg	Crocodile River	Quince, R. (11)	ET	,50	1968
Scaly	Barbus natalensis	2,820 kg	Chelmsford Dam	Jenner, Thomas (15)	N	,41	1974
Cape Whitefish	Barbus andrewi	1,194 kg	Brandvlei Dam	Schneider, R.A. (15)	WP	,36	1970
Mud Mullet	Labeo umbratus	0,794 kg	Rietspruit Dam	Van Lutterveld, J. (13)	T	,42	1969
Mud-Fish Orange R.	Labeo capensis	2,500 kg	Vaal River	Stoop, C.J. (10)	ET	,35	1976
Kurper (Blue)	Tilapia mossambica	1,070 kg	Hartebeespoort Dam	Venter, M.J. (14)	T	,35	1972
Eel (Madagscar)	Anguilla marmorata	5,224 kg	Komati River	Kriel, L.D. (14)	NT	,53	1970

Index

155